Marcelo Manucci

CHANGE your life

challenging negative self talk

Visualizations
+Workbook

Copyright © 2024 by Marcelo Manucci

All rights reserved.

ISBN 9798344117294

www.marcelomanucci.com

No portion of this book may be reproduced in any form without written permission from the publisher or author, except as permitted by U.S. copyright law.

This book results from a comprehensive compilation of research and practices focused on the emotional and cognitive approach to the narratives that influence our lives. Its purpose is to provide tools and insights to enrich your internal dialogue and interactions with others, fostering greater personal well-being. However, it is essential to note that this book is not intended to replace professional therapeutic processes. If you are going through situations that require specialized attention, we recommend that you seek the support of a qualified therapist or counselor.

RESOURCES

This book allows you to read, learn, explore, and try new possibilities for dialogue, narratives, and everyday relationships. Therefore, in addition to the contents of the chapters, you will find resources at the end of the chapters that are available for download.

Visualizations for download

Throughout some chapters, you will find references to visualizations to complement your personal work. You can download the files and use these exercises as often as you need. Download the workbook using this QR code.

Workbook for download

In addition to the visualizations, you can download the worksheets for each visualization to keep track of your discoveries, achievements, and challenges. Download the workbook using this QR code.

Online Resources

At the end of the book, you will find online resources organized according to the chapter topics. These resources allow you to explore applications, free services, and software that allow you to implement meditations, narrative recordings, positive affirmations, digital boards, and other resources.

CONTENTS

Introduction	1
1. Words and Emotions	5
2. Living in Your Mind	15
3. Transform Your Landscape	25
4. Inner Dialogue	37
5. Intimate Dialogues	51
6. Social Dialogues	61
7. Difficult Dialogues	67
8. Virtual Dialogues	79
9. Toxic Narratives	93
10. An Optimistic View	101
11. Hidden Mandates	111
12. Uncertainty	119
13. Next Steps	125
14. Online Resources	129
Thank you!	133
15. References	135

INTRODUCTION
Transforming experiences

In the mid-19th century, when the first Neanderthal fossils were unearthed, scientists marveled at the striking similarities between the skulls of these ancient beings and modern human skulls. This discovery illuminated a profound connection, revealing that these ancient humans, who vanished over 40,000 years ago, possessed brain characteristics remarkably similar to ours. Despite their smaller and more robust bodies, they shared with us a complexity of thought and an ability to create symbols beyond mere survival. Recent dating techniques have even shown that Neanderthals were the creators of cave paintings around 65,000 years ago, indicating they, too, possessed a form of symbolic thinking and a desire to make sense of their world.

We are a meaning-creating species, using symbols to share meanings, communicate ideas, and build relationships. This capacity for symbolization sets us apart from other mammals, allowing us to describe, explain, and justify our actions in ways that transcend primary biological responses. Human relationships are woven from this intricate web of shared meanings and personal interpretations. We do not merely react to the world; we actively shape our experiences through the symbols and narratives we create.

Throughout history, humanity has sought ever more complex ways to communicate and understand the world. From the earliest carvings on stone to our digital conversations today, dialogue has bridged our minds and hearts.

In his work *On Dialogue*, quantum physicist David Bohm delves into the transformative potential of dialogue. He suggests that it is more than just an exchange of words; it is a profound interaction that can reshape our perception of reality. Although a physicist, Bohm found deep significance in how we communicate, recognizing that subatomic particles are interconnected in unseen ways, so are we through the language and dialogues that bind us.

Why would a quantum physicist be so deeply invested in the study of dialogue? Bohm saw a parallel between the interconnectedness of particles in the quantum realm and the connections forged through human communication. In his view, dialogue explores these invisible ties that link us together. Understanding and engaging in authentic dialogue can uncover the deeper layers of reality and our place within it.

As we go through life, we carry symbols both on our bodies and within our minds. Some are overt, like ornaments, tattoos, or clothing choices. Others are more subtle, hidden in the personal mental landscapes we cultivate. We create these symbols to invite, persuade, dream, or share our inner worlds. This symbolic fabric weaves itself into the very texture of our lives, defining the space in which we exist and interact.

Evolutionarily, our brain's emotional capacity has remained relatively unchanged since the Stone Age. Our ancestors' primary emotions are those we experience today, governed by similar neurochemical responses. Thousands of years ago, a threatening animal might have triggered fear and the instinct to survive. In the medieval period, the threat might have come from societal forces like the Inquisition. Today, the sources of danger have evolved into more abstract forms—economic instability, health crises, or urban insecurity—but the emotional response remains fundamentally the same. The primal reaction to threat, whether real or perceived, still prepares us for fight or flight, echoing the survival mechanisms of our ancient forebears.

This book invites you to embark on an intimate journey into the different "mindscapes" that shape your life. It seeks to guide you in transforming and using your inner dialogues as a foundation for personal growth. Beyond the surface of mere words, it delves into the narratives that shape your emotions, thoughts, and, ultimately, your reality.

Our journey begins with exploring the inner dialogue, the ongoing monologue that continuously shapes how you perceive yourself and the world around you. This inner voice can be your greatest ally or your harshest critic. It has the power to influence your emotional well-being and steer the course of your life. Here, you will learn to recognize the immense influence of your thoughts and words on your mental state. By transforming a critical and self-deprecating inner dialogue into one that empowers and inspires, you set the stage for developing a positive mindset that fosters personal growth. This is not about dismissing or ignoring negative thoughts but engaging with them to promote self-compassion and constructive change.

Next, we will delve into intimate dialogues, those deep conversations you share with those closest to you. These dialogues are the bedrock of meaningful relationships, providing emotional support and strength during life's challenges. This section will guide you through techniques to nurture these connections, emphasizing the importance of authenticity, empathy, and vulnerability. Creating a safe space for open communication can strengthen the bonds with loved ones, fostering resilient and supportive relationships that last.

We will also explore the realm of difficult dialogues—those conversations that stir uncomfortable emotions and challenge our composure. Whether a disagreement with a friend or a challenging discussion at work, these dialogues can be the most testing. Here, you will learn strategies to stay calm and preserve dignity in the face of tension while recognizing that your words carry the power to either harm or heal. By understanding and managing your emotional reactions, you can navigate conflicts without damaging the relationships that matter to you. In this way, challenging situations can become opportunities for growth and deeper understanding.

In our increasingly digital world, the nature of dialogue has transformed. Online interactions have become a significant part of daily communication, yet they come with challenges. The chapter on virtual dialogues will provide insight into how to engage consciously in conversations on social media and other online platforms. It will offer strategies for protecting your privacy and emotional well-being in a digital age that often blurs the boundaries between personal and public life. Understanding the dynamics of online communication is crucial for maintaining a positive mindset and healthy relationships in the virtual realm.

Another critical aspect we will address is the impact of toxic narratives—those inherited beliefs and mandates that can limit your personal growth. These narratives often stem from family and cultural backgrounds, subtly influencing self-perception and choices. This chapter will guide you in questioning and redefining these inherited beliefs, freeing you from their restrictive hold. Doing so opens yourself to new possibilities and pathways for personal development, strengthening your self-esteem and building a positive mindset.

Finally, we will explore the creation of positive narratives. This chapter will teach you how the conscious choice of words can shape a healthy mental environment and foster a balanced emotional state. Drawing from neuroscientific research, you will learn how positive words and affirmations can activate chemical processes in your brain that promote well-being. Through the deliberate selection of words and engagement in transformative activities, you can cultivate a "cocktail of positive emotions" that empowers you to lead a more fulfilling life.

This book is more than a guide; it invites you to explore the depths of your dialogues and narratives. It encourages you to cleanse your mental landscape of harmful words and cultivate a fuller and more conscious life. The journey toward transformation is not instantaneous; it requires ongoing practice, dedication, and self-love. However, the rewards are profound. You deserve to live in a mental and emotional environment where every word, thought, and action contributes to your well-being and joy.

Chapter One

WORDS AND EMOTIONS

The Circuit of Meanings

Have you ever stopped to consider the words you use every day? It's an automatic process for most of us, almost like breathing. However, words are more than sounds or scribbles on a page; they are powerful symbols that shape your mental landscape. They mold your feelings, influence your actions, and ultimately define your world. In this chapter, you will discover the profound connection between language and emotions—an invisible circuit that constructs your reality. By understanding this circuit, you will learn to value the power of your words and begin the transformative journey of reshaping your inner world.

Words are not merely a means of communication; they are the foundation upon which we build our experiences. When you describe your day as "awful" or "difficult," those words directly impact your mood and how you approach the rest of the day. Language can shape perception, influence feelings, and provoke reactions. Every word you speak outwardly stems from your inner mental landscape, the narrative within your mind.

Imagine waking up on a rainy Monday after a relaxing weekend. If you tell yourself, "Today is going to be a horrible day," your brain immediately aligns with that expectation. The word "horrible" ripples your mood, affecting your energy and outlook. However, if you approach the day with an open mindset and say, "Let's see what this day has in store," you create a sense of curiosity and optimism. This is the transformative power of words in action, altering your mindset and your reality experience.

Your brain is programmed to respond to language. Hearing or reading certain words triggers emotional responses, activating a cascade of chemicals throughout your body. Consider the phrase, "This was a resounding failure." For many, these words evoke feelings of shame or disappointment. But if you replace it with, "I have something to learn here," the emotional impact shifts, and with it, your reaction to the situation. This shift can lead to a more open, growth-oriented perspective rather than a sense of defeat.

Research shows that positive language can elevate mood, while negative language can lead to frustration and defeat. Words have the power to shape our emotional responses and, in turn, our interactions with the world. This phenomenon is closely related to the "linguistic relativity hypothesis," or the "Sapir-Whorf hypothesis," which suggests that language can shape our thoughts and emotions. By consciously choosing our words, we can guide our emotional responses in a healthier, more proactive direction.

The Chemistry of Words

Using positive language can trigger the release of chemicals such as dopamine and serotonin, improving your mood, motivation, and overall well-being. Conversely, hostile or self-critical language can increase stress hormones like cortisol, leading to anxiety and depression. It's not magic; it's chemistry. By changing your vocabulary, you can alter your brain chemistry. However, this doesn't mean adopting a naive, overly optimistic stance. It's about integrating mindful language into your daily conversations to create a more balanced and constructive inner dialogue.

Your inner conversation—the constant stream of thoughts running through your mind—is the most significant dialogue you will ever have. It profoundly influences how you view yourself and the world. If this inner voice is harsh or critical, it can erode your self-esteem and hinder your ability to find fulfillment. The impact of self-talk is so significant that it can either propel you toward your goals or keep you trapped in a cycle of negativity.

To begin transforming this inner conversation, identify your words. Are they kind, supportive, and encouraging, or are they filled with doubt, criticism, and negativity? Awareness is the first step toward change. Once you identify negative patterns, you can consciously replace them with positive affirmations. For example, if you think, "I'm not good enough," change it to, "I am capable and deserving." Over time, these affirmations will reshape your self-perception and boost your confidence.

Metaphors are powerful language tools that help us understand complex concepts by relating them to familiar experiences. For instance, describing life as a "journey" allows you to see challenges as part of a grand adventure. Using positive metaphors can shift your perspective and emotions. Instead of saying, "I'm stuck," try saying, "I'm at a crossroads." This simple shift in language can open up new possibilities and reduce feelings of frustration.

Defining Boundaries with Emotions

Just as mammals define their territory with chemical secretions, humans delineate their lives' boundaries through emotions acting as chemical markers. You might recall scenes from nature documentaries where animals fight to defend their territory, underscoring how vital boundaries are to survival. In our lives, emotions limit what we consider possible, forbidden, known, and uncertain. These emotional boundaries influence our decisions and actions.

Emotions are adaptive responses that prepare us to face external or internal situations. They are essential for survival. Our brains organize a series of chemical and electrical connections that modify our body's state, priming us for action. Although emotions are triggered automatically, we are responsible for the narratives we build around them. This is where the power of words becomes apparent—our interpretation of emotions defines the boundaries we set for ourselves.

Neuroscientists identify five primary emotions: fear, sadness, joy, anger, and disgust. While some theories include secondary emotions, our responses primarily fall within these five categories. However, our interpretations of these emotions can turn fleeting feelings into prolonged emotional states of well-being or suffering. The stories we tell ourselves shape the boundaries of our mental and emotional territories.

We are, in essence, chattering mammals who define our territory chemically through emotions and deploy them in stories and interpretations. Emotional activation is a biological process beyond our control, but we can shape the narratives accompanying these emotional responses. The automatic activation of emotions is a survival resource that can trap us if we are unaware of the mental landscape we create with our daily stories and thoughts. Your brain responds to the imagery you present, whether real or imagined. Thus, your mental landscape becomes the reality your brain seeks to protect you from. It isn't that survival has turned against you; you've trained your brain to live in a state of survival through the narratives you generate daily.

The Vibrations of Words

Words are not just labels for our experiences; they are symbolic structures that construct our reality and profoundly impact our emotions and relationships. Ancient spiritual traditions, like mantras in meditation and modern science, affirm that words emit vibrations that resonate within our body and mind, influencing personal well-being and interactions with others. These positive or negative vibrations create an emotional and energetic imprint that shapes how we live our daily experiences.

A classic example of the power of words in spiritual traditions is the use of mantras. In Hinduism and Buddhism, the mantra "Om" is seen as the primordial sound of the universe, with vibrations that create harmony in both body and mind. Repeating a mantra establishes a vibratory rhythm, calming the nervous system and generating a sense of inner peace. In this context, the vibrations of words transcend their literal meaning and become tools for emotional and physical healing.

From a scientific standpoint, neurobiological studies have shown that words influence our chemical reactions. Positive words like "joy" and "love" activate the release of dopamine and oxytocin, neurotransmitters that promote well-being. In contrast, negative words such as "hate" or "fear" increase the production of cortisol, the stress hormone. This illustrates how words can shape our brain chemistry, affecting our emotions and physical health.

Consider Marta, a human resources manager who noticed her team's low morale. Instead of saying, "This is all wrong," she started using phrases like, "I want us to think about how we can improve." This subtle shift in language dramatically changed the atmosphere. Her team felt more valued and began collaborating more actively. Marta's conscious choice of words facilitated a more open and creative environment, demonstrating the power of positive language in action.

The concept of the self-fulfilling prophecy, coined by Robert K. Merton in 1948 and later expanded upon in cognitive psychology, highlights how our expectations and words influence behavior. If we tell ourselves that "something is going to go wrong," we create internal anxiety that can unconsciously steer our actions and decisions toward that negative outcome. In his book *The Art of Making Life Bitter*, Paul Watzlawick illustrates how rigid beliefs and negative language reinforce self-destructive thought patterns.

Take the case of John, a young professional who constantly repeated to himself, "I never get anything right." This limiting narrative led him to sabotage his opportunities for growth at work. When he began to use more constructive statements like, "Every day I learn something new," his self-perception changed, and he got promoted. Words that once trapped him in a cycle of negativity started to resonate in a new direction, opening doors to possibilities he hadn't imagined.

Pioneering research on the Pygmalion effect, studied by Rosenthal and Jacobson in 1968, demonstrated how expectations could shape reality. Their study revealed that students for whom teachers projected positive expectations performed better, while those with negative expectations did not fare as well. This research shows that the words we use impact ourselves and influence others, reinforcing how the vibrations of words build our relationships and outcomes.

Changing the Vibration of Words

Using colors is a creative and engaging way to change your words' vibration. Like every word emits a vibration, colors have frequencies that can alter our mood and perception. By assigning colors to your words, you can intensify the positive energy you wish to generate daily.

Here's an exercise to help you harness the power of words and colors.

Assign a Color to Each Emotion or Keyword: Imagine that the words you frequently use are tinged with specific colors. For example, choose green for "gratitude," blue for "calm," and yellow for "joy." Negative words can also have colors, like gray for "fear" or black for "hate." Assigning a color to each word helps you visualize its emotional impact, making you more aware of the vibration you create in each situation.

Transform Negative Words into Positive Ones Through Colors: Whenever you notice a negative word dominating your inner conversation, sense the darkness of its vibration. Then, transform that word into a more positive one and change its color to something more vibrant. For example, if you catch yourself saying, "I am not capable," visualize that phrase in gray. Then, change it to "I am capable," visualizing it in a bright gold or green color. This color change symbolizes the elevation of the vibration of your words.

Create a Record of Words and Colors: Track the words you use in different situations by assigning them colors. Reflect on the dominant colors in your internal and external conversations. If dark colors predominate, consciously replace those words with brighter, more vibrant ones. This exercise will help you visualize the impact of your language on your mental landscape and make more conscious choices to elevate your daily vibration.

Visualize Your Conversations with a Splash of Color: Before a meaningful conversation, close your eyes and visualize vibrantly colored words flowing between you and the other person. If you sense tension or anticipate conflict, imagine blue or green words to encourage calm and empathy. If you expect a creative exchange, visualize bright hues like yellow or orange to stimulate positive energy.

By changing the vibration of your words through colors, you can begin to transform your emotional state and the quality of your interactions. This playful approach makes you more aware of your language and allows you to experience the positive energy that words and colors combined can bring to your daily life.

Where Do Thoughts Hide?

The stable territories of everyday life are personal constructions mediated by ideas, perceptions, and emotions. In other words, you live immersed in a network of words that defines the possibilities of your actions. Every event you experience, every interaction, every unexpected situation is filtered through your thoughts and words, creating an internal narrative that gives meaning to your reality. However, this reality is a fiction constructed by you. This doesn't mean you live in delusion; it means you are the architect of your experience. By becoming aware of the thoughts supporting your fiction, you can open yourself to new experiences and explore the unknown confidently and firmly.

Before thoughts trap us, learning how to capture them is essential. Thoughts and emotions act together, molding our experiences and shaping the inner fabric of our lives. This process happens so quickly that we often find ourselves immersed in a cycle of automatic reactions, unable to stop and analyze what is happening inside us. To take control of our emotions and thoughts, it is essential to identify them and observe how they manifest themselves before they dominate our actions. Capturing these thoughts involves being attentive and aware, allowing us to decide how to respond to the emotions that arise and the narratives we feed.

Emotions play a crucial role in this plot. When confronted with new circumstances, emotions arise automatically and are covered by words that try to control or make sense of your feelings. These words, in turn, express thoughts that generate your narratives, and behind them lie the emotions that guide your reaction. Explore the words you automatically use when confronted with certain situations. You will discover that these words are connected to recurring emotions, which compulsively jump in to cover the unknown. This process often occurs unconsciously, leading to automatic responses that limit our ability to adapt.

Your arguments display the causes you create to justify what you feel or do and explain the effects of events. In this way, the scenes you recreate are connected by a causality that defines your experiences. If you can redefine these connections, you can transform how you deal with challenges. Reflect on the meaning of the arguments you tell yourself in difficult, burdensome, or frustrating situations. Exploring the causes of your feelings will allow you to find the underlying arguments that support that narrative about events. By identifying these thought patterns, you can modify them and make room for new ways of thinking and approaching events.

Similarly, your justifications define your decisions when faced with new situations. These justifications result from a deep emotional connection with the facts you interpret. What is the point of holding on to certain emotions, and why do you justify certain emotional reactions to specific events? The answer lies in an invisible emotional bond that connects words to your body. Emotions generate a chemical bond that links your words and thoughts to your body, affecting your emotional and physical state. If you explore these justifications, you will find clues to the emotional link that sustains your decisions, revealing how your thoughts are sustained bodily.

Your certainties, finally, play a vital role in the stability of your internal narrative. These certainties turn the volatile into the real and the transitory into the permanent. Often, what you assume as certainty is a mental construct that helps you make sense of the uncertainty. However, they can also be a barrier that prevents you from adapting and changing. The certainties you attach to your thoughts safeguard your sense of control in an unpredictable world. But behind them lies an uncomfortable vulnerability: fear of the unknown. As you try to maintain that control, certainties become an addiction, limiting your ability to open yourself to new experiences and perspectives.

Thinking is an automatic and unavoidable activity intricately linked with chemical processes and vibrations that occur without conscious intervention. The more we try to reject or control thoughts, the more intense they become. This is because thoughts, emotions, and words are interconnected in a complex web of energy and chemistry that defines our daily experience. Instead of fighting them, we can learn to unravel the invisible threads that bind them together to cleanse and refine our language. This way, your words are cleansed, changing your energy and creating a more stimulating mental environment.

Understanding the power of words and how they shape your mental and emotional landscape is the first step toward transformation. By acknowledging the chemistry of words and the vibrations they emit, you can begin to choose language that elevates your mood and empowers you consciously. You can redefine the narratives you live by, break free from limiting beliefs, and create a mental environment that fosters growth and fulfillment. The journey starts with a single word or thought—a simple shift in how you speak to yourself and the world around you.

Visualization

Feeling the vibration of the words

Reflect on the words you used in the visualization. Which words generated a positive vibration? Which words produced a negative vibration? List the positive words and how they affected your body and mind.

Reflection questions

What words made you feel at peace?

How did you feel the vibrations in your body change with the different words?

What emotions came up during the visualization?

How can you incorporate more positive words into your daily life?

Chapter Two

Living in Your Mind

The Web of Words and Thoughts

Our mind can feel like a labyrinth, a complex web where words and thoughts constantly interact, shaping our experiences and realities. Have you ever felt trapped in your thoughts, unable to escape a negative mindset? This chapter explores how the interplay between words and thoughts defines your daily life and how you can navigate your mental landscape more effectively by understanding and controlling this dynamic. By doing so, you cultivate a positive mindset and create a healthier, more enriching existence.

The relationship between words and thoughts is inherently circular. Words influence thoughts, and thoughts, in turn, shape the words we use. This dynamic can empower you or, conversely, create mental traps. Imagine that in a moment of doubt, you think, "I'm not good enough for this." That idea translates into words that reinforce your insecurity. The more you repeat this pattern, the stronger it becomes, creating a harmful loop that can lead to a state of inertia and perceived impossibility.

Conversely, positive words can foster healthy thoughts and strengthen a mindset driven by enthusiasm and creativity. When you start your day with affirmations like "I am capable," you set a tone of confidence and possibility.

This constant interplay between words and thoughts affects every aspect of your life. By consciously choosing your words, you influence your thoughts, breaking negative cycles and encouraging patterns that drive your development and well-being.

The Vibration of the Mind

Our thinking is not confined to what happens inside our brain; it encompasses the body and the environment we interact with. This holistic view reveals that our emotions, thoughts, and words are deeply interconnected and that our experiences are not generated in isolation. Instead, they form a dynamic vibration involving multiple dimensions of our existence. Adopting this perspective is crucial for developing a mindset that doesn't just react to circumstances but actively creates an environment conducive to personal growth.

Imagine your mind as a vast field that can be fertile and full of life or barren and gloomy. The seeds in this field are your words and thoughts, which interact with the emotions in your body and the stimuli from your environment. Every word you think or utter is a seed planted in this mental field. Depending on the nature of that seed—positive or negative—the landscape of your mind can flourish with vitality or become oppressive and dark.

When you nourish your mind with positive thoughts and constructive affirmations, you allow healthy emotions and productive actions to grow. For instance, if you believe, "I have the resources to meet this challenge," you plant seeds of confidence and resilience. Emotions of security and optimism flourish, filling your mental field with flowers of hope, motivation, and joy. This positive environment affects your feelings and extends this energy to your relationships, decisions, and actions.

In contrast, when you water your mind with negative words and ideas, such as "I will never achieve anything," these seeds of hopelessness take deep root. Emotions like fear, anxiety, and frustration emerge as weeds, stifling any potential for positive growth. Over time, these negative emotions transform your mental landscape into an oppressive space filled with self-doubt, insecurities, and constant self-criticism. This gloomy mental territory affects your behavior, causing you to avoid opportunities and relationships that could be beneficial, perpetuating a cycle of negativity that hinders your growth and well-being.

The Influence of the Environment

Your thoughts and emotions are not isolated entities; they are influenced by the people you interact with, the environments you spend time in, and the stimuli you are exposed to. The vibration of your environment also shapes the vibration of your mind. If you surround yourself with negativity—be it toxic people, cluttered spaces, or media that fuels anxiety—the vibration of your mind becomes clouded. The thoughts and words that arise in this environment are tainted, and without realizing it, your mind begins to mirror this external disarray.

Conversely, if you cultivate an environment that fosters growth—nurturing relationships, a clean and organized space, and content that promotes well-being—your mind becomes fertile ground for constructive ideas and optimistic thoughts. The interaction between the words you choose, the emotions you experience, and the environment around you is a process of constant vibration. It is your responsibility to tend to these frequencies so your mental landscape thrives.

For instance, an everyday example of this interaction can occur at work. If you constantly tell yourself, "This new role is too difficult; I can't grow," emotions of stress and frustration invade your body, tensing your muscles and accelerating your heart rate. Your thoughts become increasingly pessimistic, affecting your performance and creating a hostile mental environment where failure is inevitable. The field of your mental landscape darkens, covered with gray clouds, and every effort you make seems futile.

However, if you identify these negative seeds early and replace them with a balanced perspective, such as "This new role is challenging, so I will move forward gradually," you will notice an immediate change in your mental state. Anxiety decreases, your muscles relax, and the oppressive mental field begins to clear. Confidence strengthens, and your focus transitions to a vibration that aligns with solutions and possibilities. This transforms your emotional experience and affects the tangible results you produce.

The Bridge to Reality

Consider John, who boards public transportation every morning as the sun lights the city streets. At the subway station, John appears confident—his suit neatly pressed, briefcase in hand, ready for another day at work. But his workday began the night before when he thought about all the tasks and outcomes he needed to achieve. By the time he woke, his body was already tired because his mind had been working all night.

Although the day is bright and warm, the journey to work is very different in John's mind. As soon as he sits on the subway, his thoughts unravel into endless worries. Each thought is like a stone thrown into a pond, spreading ripples of anxiety throughout his body. In response to these vibrations, John repeats phrases to himself that only increase his tension. The list of potential problems multiplies in his mind, and with each one, his breathing becomes heavier, his muscles tense, and his heart beats harder.

The forty-minute commute becomes an internal battle as John tries to control every detail of the day ahead. "I must be prepared for every eventuality. I can't let anything go wrong today," he tells himself. Compulsive thoughts race through his mind as he tries to calm himself with even more compulsive thoughts. Locked in this mental game, John is unaware that the control he is trying to exert is a trap—a prison sustained by the very words he believes keep him safe.

By the time he arrives at the office, John is already exhausted. His mind is burdened, his body tense. He hasn't had a moment's peace since he went to bed the night before, and even though he's done nothing but sit on the subway, his energy is drained. While those around him seem to start the day with renewed energy, he feels overwhelmed by self-imposed expectations that follow him like a shadow. Still, he presses on, obedient to that inner voice that tells him everything depends on his perfection, not realizing it is that same voice slowly consuming him daily.

John is a respected and efficient professional, shaped from an early age by the expectations of his successful parents. Excellence was the minimum acceptable standard in his household, and academic and professional achievements were not just expected—they were celebrated as the only measure of success. As a child, he heard his parents talk about the importance of being the best, never settling, and always striving for more. Although his parents never overtly pressured him, the expectations were clear: John was to carry on the family tradition of success.

His career decision was almost automatic, as though a part of his path was laid out before he could question it. While John loves his profession and excels in it, he doesn't fully enjoy it. Each accomplishment, rather than being a celebration, becomes an emotional weight. Each success brings the expectation that he must surpass himself the next time. This thought pattern has become his mental trap.

Words serve as a bridge between our inner thoughts and the outside world. Words frame our daily decisions; they are the tools we use to shape our reality. Perhaps John's story resonates with you. We all have moments when our words and thoughts create a reality that may seem acceptable on the outside but is not sustainable or healthy. Self-demand, disguised as perfectionism, can stifle joy and enjoyment, turning what could be a rewarding experience into a constant burden. Through John's story, you have a mirror that allows you to recognize these internal narratives, question them, and, most importantly, transform them into a mindset that enables you to live your vocation or profession with greater freedom and satisfaction.

The Science of Narratives

The narratives we construct—the stories we tell ourselves about who we are, what we can achieve, and how we perceive the world—are intricately woven with the words we choose. This complex relationship significantly impacts our well-being and our interactions with others.

Martin Seligman, a pioneer of positive psychology, found that the language we use to describe our experiences plays a crucial role in our overall satisfaction with life. His research showed that individuals who use positive words to frame their experiences tend to experience greater happiness and possess an ability to recover from adversity. This optimism, deeply rooted in their language, generates more positive emotions and fosters resilience. When faced with challenges, they reframe difficulties as opportunities for personal growth, transforming their experiences into a source of strength rather than defeat.

Barbara Fredrickson's "broaden and build" theory further illustrates the transformative power of words. According to Fredrickson, positive emotions—and the words that evoke them—expand our awareness and enhance our problem-solving abilities. Her research demonstrates that positive language creates immediate well-being and strengthens social connections. This cycle of positive interactions builds emotional support networks, leading to healthier, more fulfilling relationships. Thus, the words we use daily do more than influence our inner experiences; they also shape our interactions with others.

Dr. John Gottman's extensive research at the University of Washington revealed the profound impact of language on relationships, particularly in couples. Gottman discovered that couples who consistently use positive language in their interactions are likelier to maintain a stable and happy relationship over time. He accurately predicted whether a couple would stay together or break up based on the ratio of positive to negative interactions.

The Physical Impact of Words

The influence of words extends beyond our mental and emotional states; they can also have a measurable physiological impact. Recent studies indicate that using positive words can reduce cortisol levels, the hormone associated with stress. Conversely, negative words tend to elevate cortisol levels, leading to increased anxiety and physical tension. This phenomenon is evident on an individual level and within social contexts. Interactions filled with positive words create more harmonious environments, reducing stress and fostering empathy among people.

This interplay between language and physiology is part of a more extensive, more intricate system. When we use positive words, they act as catalysts that trigger the release of neurotransmitters like dopamine and oxytocin, which contribute to feelings of pleasure, trust, and bonding. This hormonal shift enhances our mood and primes our body to respond to challenges more effectively, fostering resilience and emotional stability.

Beyond emotional and physical effects, the narratives we create can reshape our brains on a neurological level. Neuroscience has shown that when we repeatedly use positive words and affirmations, our brains begin forming new neural pathways reinforcing these thought patterns. This process, known as neuroplasticity, is the brain's ability to reorganize itself by forming new neural connections throughout life. By consistently choosing a positive language, we can effectively rewire our brains to adopt a more constructive and optimistic outlook. Over time, these new narratives become habitual, creating a foundation for healthier mental habits and enhancing our overall well-being.

The science of narratives suggests that we are not passive observers of our lives; we are the authors of our own stories. We can reshape our mental and emotional landscape by consciously altering our language to describe ourselves and our experiences. This change can lead to a more balanced, fulfilling, and meaningful life. The narratives we craft determine how we feel in the present and influence our future, opening up new opportunities and fostering more rewarding relationships.

To harness the power of words in creating a more enriching and fulfilling life, consider integrating the following practices into your daily routine.

Conscious Thought: Begin by paying close attention to the connection between your thoughts and the words you use. You may find a direct, almost magical relationship when you start changing certain words in your thoughts and observe the effects on your mindset. Practice replacing self-limiting language with words that empower and uplift you. Notice how this slight shift can ripple impact on your overall mental state.

Reframe Negative Narratives: Challenge negative thoughts by reframing them with positive or neutral alternatives. Instead of viewing setbacks as failures, reframe them as learning experiences or stepping stones toward growth. By consciously changing the narrative, you can alter your perception and reduce the emotional impact of negative events, improving your overall well-being.

Change Affirmations: Incorporate positive affirmations into your daily routine to reinforce constructive thought patterns. Repeat these affirmations regularly to develop the habit of speaking kindly to yourself. Many of us have been conditioned to internalize criticism, but we can transform our internal dialogue by treating ourselves with appreciation and compassion. This positive self-talk can extend outward, enhancing our interactions with others and fostering healthier relationships.

Rescue the Positive: Make it a habit to focus on what you are grateful for each day. Practicing gratitude helps you shift your attention from what is lacking to what is abundant in your life. By actively seeking out and acknowledging the positive aspects of your experiences, even amid adversity, you cultivate a mindset that is resilient and open to growth.

Cultivating Your Narratives

Emotions are dynamic, and our language should reflect this complexity. Adopting a mindful approach to your words can cultivate a more vibrant and balanced emotional life. Living inside your mind can be intricate and challenging, but understanding the interplay between words and thoughts allows you to navigate this internal landscape with greater creativity and optimism. By being aware of your language and thought patterns, you can make conscious choices that foster a positive and fulfilling existence.

To further explore the power of narratives, engage in a creative activity that treats your mental territory like a garden. You can build this garden on a piece of cardboard, a whiteboard, or a virtual board. This exercise aims to visually and practically redefine your mental narratives, transforming them into a healthier and more constructive mental space.

Identify Your Mental Weeds: Draw a garden with several pots or plots, each representing an area of your life (e.g., work, relationships, health). In each plot, write down the negative thoughts or words you habitually use—these are your mental weeds. These might be limiting beliefs or harmful perspectives that clutter your mental landscape. Highlight them using dark colors to signify their impact.

Clean Up the Garden: Replace these mental weeds with new, positive, or neutral narratives written on separate cards. These represent the plants or flowers you want to cultivate in your mental garden. Place these new narratives in your garden, symbolizing the process of planting healthier thoughts instead of negative ones.

Renew the Affirmations: Choose three of the most potent positive affirmations from your new narratives and place them in a special, visible spot (e.g., on mirrors, in a diary, on a refrigerator magnet). Decorate these affirmations with colors and images that inspire you. Whenever you encounter negative thoughts, return to these affirmations and repeat them aloud, visualizing them growing and thriving in your mental garden.

Contemplate Your New Garden: At the end of each day, review the new narratives you've planted. Reflect on how they have influenced your thoughts and emotions throughout the day. Add a new card each day with something positive you've experienced. This could be a lesson learned, an act of kindness, or something you're grateful for. These cards act as mental nutrients, nurturing your garden with positive energy.

Visualization

Identifying mental weeds

Reflect on the mental weeds you identified in your garden. Describe these weeds and note how you pulled them out and what you planted in their place.

Reflection questions

What negative emotions or thoughts were associated with those weeds?
How did it feel to replace them with new seeds of positive thinking?
How has your mental garden changed after this visualization?

Chapter Three

TRANSFORM YOUR LANDSCAPE

The Power of Visualizations

Your mind is not merely a repository for thoughts and words; it is a canvas on which narratives and visualizations take shape, influencing how you perceive the world and navigate daily life. These stories and images are not static—they actively shape your emotions, guide your decisions, and define your experiences. In this chapter, you will explore the integration of narratives and visualizations as tools to transform your mental landscape, creating a more transparent and more positive view of everyday life.

Narratives are the stories we tell ourselves about who we are, what we can accomplish, and how we perceive our surroundings. These stories serve as a framework for understanding the world and give meaning to our experiences. Reflect for a moment: what stories do you tell yourself? Are they narratives that highlight your strengths and potential, or do they focus on limitations and setbacks? Recognizing these internal stories is the first step toward transforming them.

As symbolic mammals, we create mental situations through our emotions and the narratives we construct around them. These two dimensions—emotions and narratives—influence our perceptions and determine our actions. Ultimately, we do not react solely to facts; we respond to the mental representations we create based on our perceptions and emotions. These emotional responses are often automatic, affecting how we interpret situations and guide our behavior.

Facts are events that happen in the external world, but the circumstances we face are mental recreations of those facts. We experience life not through direct contact with reality but through the mental images we construct. When your mental landscape becomes oppressive or threatening, it is not necessarily the external situation causing this distress but instead your internal representation of it. To break free from this cycle, you need to recreate your internal references—changing emotions, thoughts, perceptions, and habits—to expand your repertoire of responses to situations.

Transformation Codes

While we cannot change external facts, we have the power to modify our emotional, cognitive, and perceptual perspectives. This internal shift allows us to respond to situations more effectively. Our mental landscape is a compilation of references from our personal history, reused in every new experience. These references shape our emotional states, influencing whether we experience joy or suffering. It is essential to realize that these states reflect our historical references.

A key code for accessing the transformation of your landscape is language—the symbolic fabric that gives meaning and value to your daily experiences. Every word you choose has the power to alter your perception of events and the emotions you experience. When you change your narrative, you change the internal references that guide you, opening up new ways of responding to life's challenges.

Emotions form another critical layer of this transformation code. If words provide the structure and shape of your mental landscape, emotions infuse it with color and tone, determining how you experience it. For example, approaching a situation with a negative emotional state can obscure your vision, leading to paranoid or defensive thoughts. Your narrative then focuses on the darker aspects of the situation, and your actions become geared solely toward survival. Conversely, a positive emotional perspective opens up new possibilities. Emotions such as trust, gratitude, and hope act as filters that enrich your mental landscape, offering a broader view of the opportunities at hand.

Visualizations are powerful tools for transforming your mental landscape because they integrate language and emotions to create a more positive reality. They make the words you choose vivid images that evoke positive emotions, contributing to a healthier mental environment. Visualization is more than just imagining; it is about creating an internal experience that can redefine the landmarks of your landscape.

By practicing visualization, you consciously connect with your emotions, using images representing possibilities, strengths, and solutions. This practice helps you use your words and emotions to shape your inner reality, leading to greater well-being and balance. Visualizations empower you to change the tonal quality of your mental landscape, allowing you to navigate life with more openness and creativity.

The Hidden Paths of Your Landscape

Every mental landscape contains hidden pathways—unrecognized, underestimated, or ignored references that guide your automatic responses. These hidden aspects shape how you approach situations and often go unnoticed, influencing your reactions without your awareness. However, identifying and transforming these hidden pathways can change how you perceive and respond to challenges.

Explore Your Emotions: Identify the emotions that arise in specific situations. What words or events trigger these emotions? How do they manifest in your body? Recognizing these patterns is the first step to understanding and altering them.

Examine Associated Narratives: Reflect on the thoughts accompanying these emotions. What arguments support the narrative? Are these thoughts based on facts, or can they be reinterpreted with alternative perspectives? By questioning these narratives, you can begin to rewrite them.

Analyze Your Perceptions: Consider what you see around you. Are your interpretations the only possible, or do underlying emotions influence them? Challenge your perceptions to reveal the full spectrum of reality.

Explore Your Options for Action: Assess the responses available to you in a given situation. Are they your only options, or have you overlooked alternatives due to ingrained narratives? Expanding your view of possible actions can lead to more creative solutions.

By exploring the references in your mental landscape, you become aware of the subjective images you've constructed. The landscape is colored by emotions that affect how you perceive events and act. Depending on your emotional state, it can appear vibrant and dynamic or dark and oppressive.

The Science of Visualizations

One of the most effective ways to alter the nuances of your mental landscape is through visualization. This technique involves creating detailed mental images of desired outcomes or scenarios you want to experience. Visualization is more than wishful thinking—it is a method of preparing your mind to handle situations more clearly and confidently.

Scientific studies have shown that when we visualize success, our brains process it like a real experience, building the neural connections necessary to turn that vision into reality. This process, known as "mental rehearsal," explains why visualization effectively enhances performance and achieves goals.

Visualization is not merely a motivational exercise but a technique grounded in neuroscience. Studies reveal that visualization activates the same brain regions as performing a physical activity or experiencing a real-life situation. This overlap is why mental rehearsal is so effective—it allows the brain to practice and refine actions, thoughts, and responses in a safe, controlled environment.

Dr. Pascual-Leone at Harvard University conducted a pioneering study where participants imagined playing the piano. Remarkably, the brain areas responsible for movement and coordination were activated in the same way as if they were physically playing the instrument. Participants who only imagined playing showed significant improvement in their skills, almost as much as those who practiced physically. This finding suggests that the brain does not differentiate between physical action and mental representation, making visualization a powerful substitute for physical practice.

A similar study at the University of Chicago involved athletes mentally rehearsing free throws in basketball. After several weeks, the athletes who had only used visualization improved their skills by a similar percentage to those who physically practiced. This reinforces that visualization can enhance physical performance because the brain treats mental practice as real training.

Visualization's impact extends beyond improving physical skills; it also induces changes in brain structure. A study conducted at Ohio University in 2007 revealed that visualization can lead to neuroplasticity, the brain's ability to reorganize and form new neural connections. By imagining an activity or goal, the brain activates the corresponding regions and strengthens the synaptic connections related to that activity. Over time, mental practice can transform the brain's structure, making executing the visualized actions more fluid and natural.

Beyond its physical and neurological benefits, visualization has a profound emotional and motivational component. A study published in *Neuroscience* in 2013 showed that visualizing personal goals activates the brain's reward system, releasing dopamine, the neurotransmitter associated with pleasure and motivation. This dopamine release helps maintain energy and enthusiasm toward achieving goals. Participants who visualized their goals in detail reported higher levels of motivation and commitment, which translated into a higher likelihood of realizing those goals.

To maximize the benefits of visualization, practice it regularly. Studies suggest that spending a few minutes daily visualizing your goals can strengthen the neural pathways associated with those goals and sustain your motivation. Visualizing your objectives with detail and excitement primes your brain to pursue them as if they have already been achieved. The brain reorganizes its neural connections to pay attention, focus, and process events based on what you highlight as necessary in your visualization.

Techniques for Effective Visualization

Practicing it regularly and with intention is essential to harness the full potential of visualization. Visualization is not simply daydreaming or wishful thinking; it is about creating a focused, immersive mental experience that can influence your mindset and behavior. Here are key techniques to help you create compelling visualizations.

Create a Clear Picture: Create a detailed mental image of the scene or goal you want to achieve. This involves more than just a vague outline—be specific and vivid in your imagination. Include the environment, people, colors, sounds, and smells associated with the situation. The clearer and more detailed the image, the more impact it will have on your subconscious mind.

Involve All Your Senses: To make your visualization more powerful, engage all your senses. Don't just see the scene; feel the emotions, hear the sounds, and even smell the scents involved. For instance, imagine the feel of the clicker in your hand, the sound of applause, and the room's warmth if you're visualizing a successful presentation. This multisensory approach creates a more immersive experience, making the mental image more convincing and impactful.

Practice Consistently: Visualization is a skill that improves with regular practice. Set aside a few minutes each day to practice. The more you visualize, the more you strengthen the neural pathways associated with your goals. Consistency is critical to making visualization an effective tool for transformation.

Introduce Positive Emotions: Incorporating positive emotions is crucial to effective visualization. As you visualize your desired outcome, consciously evoke joy, pride, confidence, and satisfaction. These emotions enhance the mental image and make it more real to your subconscious mind, reinforcing the belief that you can achieve your goals.

The Mandala of Transformation

Creating a transformation mandala is one creative and powerful way to integrate visualization into your practice. The mandala, "circle" in Sanskrit, has been used for centuries in various spiritual and ritual contexts. It serves as a tool for meditation, introspection, and personal transformation, reflecting the universe's unity, balance, and wholeness.

Creating a transformation mandala can be a profound exercise in manifesting your visualizations. It allows you to translate your mental images into a physical form, making your goals and aspirations tangible. Creating and contemplating your mandala helps you focus your intentions, release negative energies, and connect with your inner purpose.

1. Visualize Your Scene: Take a few minutes to visualize a specific situation or goal you wish to transform. This could be a professional achievement, a personal challenge, or an emotional state you want to change. Sit in a quiet place, close your eyes, and imagine this situation in detail. See the colors, feel the emotions, hear the sounds, and consider the potential outcomes. Don't limit yourself to visualizing only the result—focus on the journey, the steps you'll take, the celebrations along the way, and how this transformation will affect other areas of your life.

2. Create the Mandala: After your visualization, begin creating your mandala. This mandala will be a visual and symbolic representation of your transformation process.

- **Choose Your Base**: Select a base for your mandala, such as a canvas, cardboard, or a digital platform. Draw a large circle in the center, serving as the container for your visualizations.

- **Select Colors**: Choose colors representing the emotions and mental states you wish to embody. For example, blue might symbolize calm, green for renewal, and red for passion. Use these colors throughout your mandala to reflect the emotional tones of your visualization.

- **Integrate Symbols**: Add symbols that resonate with your transformation journey. These could be universal symbols like the sun for energy and rebirth or personal symbols like an amulet representing protection or strength. Place these symbols strategically within the mandala to signify different stages or elements of your journey.

- **Incorporate Personal Elements**: Use photos, clippings, or drawings representing your goals and dreams. Include images of moments when you felt successful or joyful. These tangible elements ground your mandala in reality and remind you what you have already accomplished and what you aspire to achieve.

   - **Write Inspirational Words**: Incorporate words into your mandala that inspire and motivate you. These words should be aligned with your goals and the emotions you want to evoke. For instance, use words like "strength," "possibility," "courage," and "growth." Write them in bright, attractive colors and place them strategically within the mandala. This practice helps replace limiting thoughts with empowering ones.

3. Connect with Your Mandala: Once your mandala is complete, place it somewhere you can see it regularly. Your mandala is not just a piece of art but a living, evolving reflection of your journey. Spend a few minutes each day connecting with it. Sit quietly before it, take deep breaths, and let the colors, symbols, and words reconnect you with your original visualizations. Whenever you face a challenging situation or need motivation, revisit your mandala to draw inspiration and strength.

4. Evolve Your Mandala: Feel free to modify your mandala as you progress on your journey. Add new elements, change colors, or add symbols representing new goals or milestones. Your mandala is a dynamic representation of your transformation and should evolve with you.

The power of the mandala lies in its ability to mirror one's inner state. By engaging in this creative process, one externalizes one's internal experiences, making them tangible and accessible. Creating a mandala is meditative, fostering mental balance, releasing negative energies, and promoting inner calm.

Modern studies support the therapeutic effects of mandala creation. Engaging with mandalas has been shown to reduce stress, improve focus, and facilitate emotional regulation. This practice provides a structured yet flexible means of exploring and transforming the mind's landscape.

Visualization as a Daily Practice

Integrating visualization into your daily routine can be a transformative experience. Here's how you can incorporate it seamlessly.

Morning Visualizations: Begin your day with a short visualization session. Spend a few minutes visualizing how you want your day to unfold. Imagine navigating through challenges confidently and easily, achieving your goals, and ending the day with a sense of accomplishment. This sets a positive tone for the day and primes your mind to be proactive and solution-oriented.

Midday Check-ins: Take brief moments throughout your day to visualize success in specific tasks or interactions. Imagine a positive outcome, whether it's an important meeting, a presentation, or a conversation. This quick mental rehearsal can boost your confidence and focus.

Evening Reflections: End your day with a visualization reflecting your progress. Visualize the day's successes, no matter how small, and imagine how they contribute to your overall goals. Use this time to visualize the steps you'll take tomorrow to build on today's achievements.

Regular visualization can rewire your brain, making pursuing your goals more natural and attainable. As you continue to practice visualization, you'll find it easier to navigate challenges, stay focused on your objectives, and maintain a positive outlook.

Moving Beyond Visualization

While visualization is a powerful tool for transformation, it's essential to integrate it with action. Visualization prepares your mind and body for success, but taking concrete steps toward your goals is what ultimately turns those visualizations into reality. Think of visualization as the mental rehearsal for the performance of life—it sets the stage, but the real work happens in the actions you take each day.

Set Clear Intentions: Use your visualizations to clarify your intentions. What do you want to achieve, and what steps will you take to get there? Visualization can help you see the path more clearly, but you must walk it.

Take Small Steps: After each visualization session, identify one small action to move closer to your goal. No matter how small, these actions will reinforce your created mental images and build momentum toward achieving your objectives.

Reflect and Adjust: As you take action, use your visualizations to reflect on your progress and make adjustments. Visualization is not a static process; it's a dynamic tool that evolves with you. Use it to stay connected to your goals, celebrate successes, and adapt to obstacles.

Your mental landscape is not fixed; it is a living, evolving space you can shape. Integrating positive narratives and visualizations into your daily life allows you to create a mental environment that supports your growth, well-being, and fulfillment. This transformation takes time, practice, and dedication, but the rewards are profound—a more harmonious mental environment, greater resilience, and a more prosperous emotional life.

The journey to transforming your mental landscape begins with small, conscious changes in how you think, feel, and visualize. As you practice these techniques, you will notice a shift in how you perceive and respond to the world around you. You'll find that your mental landscape becomes a place of possibility and creativity, where challenges are growth opportunities and where the seeds of your aspirations can take root and flourish.

Visualizations

Overcoming a challenge/ Empowering a project/ Overcoming a difficult situation

Reflection questions

Visualization to overcome a challenge. Reflect on the emotions that arose and how you feel now.

What steps did you visualize to overcome it?
How did it feel to reach the top of the mountain?
What did you learn about your ability to overcome challenges?

Visualization to enhance a project. Describe the fruits that this project produced. How did you take care of it and make it grow?

What care and attention did you give it during the visualization?
What fruits did your project bear in the visualization?
How can you apply what you learned in visualization to real life?

Visualization to overcome a difficult situation from the past. Analyze how you feel now that the situation is behind you.

How did it feel to see the dark cloud dissipate?
What positive emotions arose when the sun appeared?
How do you feel about the situation now?

Chapter Four

INNER DIALOGUE

The Stage of Your Mind

Our minds constantly engage in internal dialogues, those intimate conversations that weave together our thoughts, recover scenes from the past and create projections for the future. These inner dialogues play a central role in shaping our perception of the world and, more importantly, how we perceive ourselves. In this chapter, we will explore the immense power of your inner dialogue, how it influences your self-esteem, and, most crucially, how you can transform it to cultivate a healthier mental landscape.

The internal conversation is more than a simple reflection of passing thoughts. It is an active force that impacts your daily experience, emotions, and behavior. The monologue that unfolds in your mind throughout the day—whether positive, neutral, or critical—creates a narrative that empowers or limits you.

Imagine a typical scenario: you've missed an essential detail at work or made a mistake. The inner dialogue that follows can take two forms. If your mind reacts with, "How could I be so stupid? I never do anything right," it drags you into a spiral of self-doubt and anxiety. Alternatively, if your response is, "I made a mistake; how can I learn from it and move forward?" your inner dialogue becomes a tool for growth and resilience. In this way, your self-talk doesn't just reflect your thoughts—it actively shapes them and creates the emotional context in which you operate.

Over time, repeated negative dialogue starts to solidify as part of your identity. If you consistently tell yourself, "I'm not good at this," that belief becomes an emotional and mental reality. This leads to avoidance of challenges and reinforces feelings of inadequacy. However, by deliberately shifting your inner dialogue to statements like, "This is difficult, but I'll find a way to handle it," you cultivate confidence and proactive behaviors that allow you to rise above obstacles. Inner dialogue is not passive; it's the foundation of your actions and emotions, and you can transform it.

The Emotional Impact of Inner Dialogue

Your inner dialogue is closely tied to your emotions, and negative self-talk can create a powerful feedback loop that intensifies feelings of anxiety, fear, or shame. When you engage in critical self-talk, you reinforce negative emotions, leading to behaviors that reflect those emotions. This cycle can result in a chronic sense of inadequacy or helplessness.

For example, a common phrase like "I always mess things up" creates a mental narrative that perpetuates feelings of failure. These thoughts don't just stay in the mind's abstract realm—they also affect your body. When you're stuck in a loop of negative thinking, you may notice tension in your muscles, headaches, or feelings of fatigue. Your brain processes these thoughts as real threats, releasing stress hormones like cortisol, which intensify the physical sensations of anxiety.

Conversely, positive inner dialogue can reduce stress and cultivate feelings of confidence, calm, and optimism. When you speak to yourself kindly, your brain releases chemicals like serotonin and dopamine, which promote well-being and emotional balance. It's not just about being mindlessly optimistic; it's about giving yourself the mental space to handle challenges with resilience and self-compassion.

Cultivating a more compassionate inner dialogue doesn't mean ignoring problems or pretending everything is fine. It means shifting your mindset to one that encourages learning, growth, and emotional regulation. By transforming how you talk to yourself, you can create a healthier emotional landscape that empowers you to navigate life's challenges more effectively.

Recognizing Negative Inner Dialogue

The first step in transforming your internal dialogue is recognizing when it has turned negative. This is not always easy, as negative self-talk can be subtle and deeply ingrained. You might not even be aware of the constant stream of criticism running through your mind. However, you'll notice how frequently these thoughts arise once you pay attention.

Negative inner dialogue often manifests as absolute, exaggerated statements like, "I always fail" or "I'm not good enough." These sweeping generalizations are untrue and damaging, reinforcing beliefs that limit your potential. Over time, these thoughts become habitual, and you start to accept them as part of who you are, even though they are distorted and incomplete versions of reality.

To begin recognizing negative inner dialogue, practice mindful awareness of your thoughts. Pay attention to the moments when you are self-critical or feel emotionally low. Try to pinpoint the specific words and phrases you use. For example, if you notice yourself thinking, "I'll never be able to do this," pause and reflect on whether that thought is based on fact or fear. Writing down these negative thoughts can also help bring them into clearer focus. By making your internal dialogue visible, you gain a sense of distance from it, allowing you to see it more objectively.

Once you become aware of the negative patterns in your inner dialogue, you can challenge and change them. The goal is not to replace negative thoughts with overly positive or unrealistic ones but to adopt more balanced, realistic, and constructive self-talk. For instance, instead of saying, "I always mess up," try saying, "I made a mistake this time, but I can learn from it and improve." This slight shift reframes the narrative, allowing you to move forward with self-compassion and confidence.

Shifting from Criticism to Compassion

Developing a compassionate inner dialogue is about learning to treat yourself with the same kindness and understanding you would offer a close friend. Often, we are much harsher with ourselves than we would ever be with someone else. If a friend came to you feeling down after making a mistake, you wouldn't tell them they were a failure or unworthy—you'd offer support, encouragement, and perspective. Why do we speak to ourselves in ways we never talk to others?

One practical way to develop compassionate self-talk is to imagine what you would say to a friend in a similar situation and then direct those words toward yourself. For example, if your inner dialogue says, "You're not good enough," counter it by asking yourself, "Would I say this to someone I care about?" The answer is likely no. Instead, tell yourself, "I'm doing my best, and it's okay to make mistakes. I'll keep learning and improving."

Another technique to foster self-compassion is to keep a journal to reflect on your inner dialogue daily. In this journal, write down moments when you were particularly hard on yourself and then rewrite those moments with compassion. For example, if you wrote, "I failed that presentation, and now everyone thinks I'm incompetent," revise it to say, "I didn't present as well as I hoped, but that doesn't define my abilities. I'll use this as a learning experience to improve next time." Writing helps reinforce positive, compassionate thoughts and rewires your brain to adopt a healthier inner dialogue.

It's important to remember that self-compassion is not about letting yourself off the hook or avoiding accountability. It's about acknowledging that you are human, that everyone makes mistakes, and that your failures do not define your worth. This mindset creates a foundation of emotional resilience, making it easier to navigate challenges without succumbing to self-criticism.

One of the most effective ways to shift your inner dialogue is through the regular use of positive affirmations. Affirmations are statements that reflect the reality you want to create. By repeating affirmations consistently, you begin to reprogram your mind, replacing negative self-talk with empowering thoughts that support your goals and well-being.

For affirmations to be effective, they need to resonate with you. Choosing affirmations that feel authentic and aligned with your values is essential. For example, instead of saying, "I'm perfect and never make mistakes," which can feel unrealistic, try something like, "I'm capable of growth and learning from every experience." This kind of affirmation acknowledges your humanity while encouraging progress.

Write your affirmations down and place them where you can see them daily—on your mirror, phone, or computer screen. Repeating these statements is a gentle reminder to approach yourself with kindness and confidence. Over time, these affirmations will shape your inner dialogue, allowing positive thoughts to become your default response rather than critical or defeatist ones.

Dialogue and Identity

Your inner dialogue forms the core of your identity. It's not just a reflection of how you see yourself in the moment but shapes your long-term self-concept. Through this internal dialogue, the narratives you tell yourself build a framework that influences everything from your confidence to your sense of belonging. Think about it: if you constantly tell yourself, "I'm not good enough," this belief eventually hardens into part of your identity. It becomes an invisible filter through which you view every situation, relationship, and opportunity.

Over time, these internal narratives determine your behavior. If your inner dialogue tells you, "I'm always going to fail," you're more likely to avoid risks, withdraw from challenges, and close yourself off growth opportunities. This avoidance reinforces the original negative belief, perpetuating a cycle of limitation. The mind works to confirm its narrative, even if it is harmful.

On the other hand, if your internal monologue reflects a more positive, balanced perspective—"I have the skills to handle this challenge," or "I'm capable of learning and growing"—your behavior will align with these empowering beliefs. You'll be more inclined to engage in opportunities, persist through difficulties, and ultimately shape a life that mirrors these constructive inner thoughts.

This is why nurturing a healthy, empowering inner dialogue is essential. Positive self-talk reinforces a positive identity, while negative self-talk can sabotage your confidence and sense of self-worth. Shifting the internal dialogue alters how you feel and fundamentally redefines who you believe you are.

Regarding identity, inner dialogue isn't just passive commentary—it actively constructs the narrative of who you are. You can reshape that narrative and your life by consciously choosing to rewrite the script.

Start by questioning the negative beliefs you hold about yourself. For instance, if you tell yourself, "I'm not good at public speaking," ask yourself whether this belief is based on experience or simply fear. Have you failed every time you've spoken in public, or did you have one bad experience that left a strong impression? Maybe you've never really tried public speaking and are basing your self-criticism on imagined fears. By challenging these beliefs, you unravel the layers of negative identity you've built up over time.

Next, reframe these beliefs into more constructive ones. Instead of saying, "I'm not good at public speaking," try, "I'm still learning to be comfortable speaking in public, and with practice, I will improve." This reframe shifts your identity from one of inadequacy to one of potential. It opens up space for growth, learning, and self-compassion, allowing you to engage with new challenges rather than retreat from them.

Learning to regulate your emotions is vital to maintaining a healthy internal dialogue. Your thoughts about yourself are closely tied to how you feel, and this emotional connection can either reinforce or dismantle your identity.

For instance, when you feel anxious or stressed, your inner dialogue often mirrors those emotions with thoughts like, "I can't handle this" or "I'm not strong enough." These thoughts, in turn, intensify the emotional response, creating a feedback loop that reinforces the negative identity. However, by learning to manage your emotions—through mindfulness, deep breathing, or simply pausing to reflect—you can interrupt this loop and take control of your inner dialogue.

When you're in a disturbed emotional state, take a moment to pause and ask yourself: "What story am I telling myself right now? Is it based on facts or a reaction to my current feelings?" This awareness can help you separate your emotions from your identity. Just because you feel overwhelmed in the moment doesn't mean you are incapable. By reframing the inner dialogue, you can shift your emotional state and, over time, reinforce a more positive self-concept.

These internal conversations unfold in the stage of your mind, shaping the story of who you are and who you believe yourself to be. By taking conscious control of these dialogues and learning to regulate the emotions that fuel them, you can reshape your internal world and how you experience life.

The Unexpected Mirror

The story of Jeanne provides a vivid example of how our inner dialogue can define our reality and, more importantly, how an unexpected moment of reflection can spark profound transformation.

Jeanne was entering a stage of her life where her sense of maturity and self-reflection had grown. She was successful in her career and respected by her colleagues, yet there was an undercurrent of loneliness and dissatisfaction. Despite her achievements, Jeanne couldn't shake the feeling that something was missing. She longed for deeper connections, but her relationships never seemed to work out as she'd hoped. As time passed, her frustration grew, and her inner dialogue became more critical and self-defeating.

Jeanne's internal landscape was filled with negativity. She often criticized herself and others, and her thoughts were constantly focused on what was wrong in her life. This critical lens distorted her perceptions, leaving her in a cycle of reproach and pessimism. While she maintained close friendships, even her friends noticed how biting negativity had replaced her once optimistic personality. Although sometimes amusing, Jeanne's sharp critiques of others often ended conversations sourly. What started as lighthearted banter gradually became a toxic habit that deepened her sense of isolation.

As Jeanne's inner dialogue grew harsher, her physical and emotional well-being began to suffer. She was frequently tired, her body felt tense, and she often experienced headaches. Her pessimistic thoughts were weighing her down, not just mentally but physically as well. Her body was manifesting the tension and stress caused by her constant inner criticism.

One winter afternoon, after a heated argument at work over a trivial matter, Jeanne felt the total weight of her inner dialogue collapse on her. An overwhelming wave of anxiety washed over her, leaving her short of breath, her hands trembling, and her heart racing. Tears welled up in her eyes, and she felt as though she couldn't breathe. For the first time, Jeanne realized that her internal critic had reached a breaking point.

Leaving work early that day, Jeanne sought refuge in a nearby park, hoping for peace. Sitting on a bench, she watched the world go by, her mind still swirling with critical thoughts. As she sat there, she overheard a conversation from a nearby bench. A woman was on the phone, venting her frustrations about everything—from the weather to her job and relationships. Every word she spoke was a complaint, filled with negativity and blame.

At first, Jeanne paid little attention, but as the woman's words continued, something shifted. Jeanne began to recognize the tone, the cadence, and the relentless criticism in the woman's voice—it was eerily similar to her inner dialogue. The woman's complaints echoed the very things Jeanne often told herself, and in that moment, she was struck by a realization: this stranger's words mirrored her internal world. Jeanne had been speaking to herself in the same destructive way for years, and hearing it from someone else made her painfully aware of the damage it was causing.

This moment of clarity was a turning point for Jeanne. For the first time, she saw her inner critic for what it was: a distorted, unhelpful voice holding her back. The woman's complaints, once just background noise, had become a mirror reflecting Jeanne's inner turmoil. It was a moment of revelation that changed everything.

Jeanne realized that if she continued down this path, she would remain trapped in a cycle of negativity, disconnected from her potential and the people who cared about her. That evening, she contacted her friends and shared her experience, opening up about the critical voice dominating her thoughts. To her surprise, her friends responded with compassion and understanding, reassuring her that they believed in her ability to change.

From that day forward, Jeanne committed herself to transforming her inner dialogue. She became more mindful of her words when talking to herself, focusing on positive affirmations and realistic self-assessments. She began journaling and reflecting on the patterns that had trapped her for so long. Slowly, her inner critic lost its power, replaced by a kinder, more compassionate voice.

Jeanne's journey wasn't easy, and the transformation didn't happen overnight. But with consistent effort, she noticed subtle changes in her mood, energy levels, and even her physical well-being. The tension in her body gradually eased, her headaches became less frequent, and her friends remarked on how much lighter and more joyful she seemed. The negative, critical woman she had once been was fading, replaced by a more empowered, confident version of herself.

Jeanne's story is a powerful reminder of how our inner dialogue can shape our reality—and how, with conscious effort, we can change it. Jeanne could rewrite her story by recognizing the destructive nature of her inner critic and deciding to shift her self-talk. Her journey shows us that transformation is always possible, no matter how deeply ingrained our negative beliefs may be.

Unmask Your Inner Critic

The final part of this chapter focuses on a practical, creative exercise designed to help you identify, personify, and challenge your inner critic. By visualizing and giving a tangible form to the critical voice inside your head, you can distance yourself from its harsh judgments, confront its messages, and ultimately weaken its influence over your life. The key to this process is bringing awareness to the inner critic so you can learn to differentiate between its voice and your true self.

1. Meet Your Inner Critic: The first step in this exercise is to identify your inner critic. This may initially seem simple, but recognizing the critic's voice requires mindfulness and attention. It often lurks in the background, subtly influencing your thoughts without you even realizing it. Your inner critic might manifest as self-doubt, harsh judgments, or negative assumptions about your abilities. The voice says, "You're not good enough," or "You'll never succeed."

Find a quiet place where you can reflect without distractions. Sit comfortably, close your eyes, and allow yourself to think about moments when your inner critic has been loudest. Perhaps it emerges when you're about to take on a new challenge, start a new project, or face a difficult conversation. Notice the exact words it uses—are they repetitive, cruel, or diminishing?

What emotions arise when your inner critic speaks? Fear, shame, or guilt? These emotions are vital to recognizing the critic's presence.

Once you've identified the tone and nature of your inner critic, take a moment to personify it. Imagine that this voice has a shape, a form, or a character. Does it have a specific look? Is it a small, sneering figure or a significant, domineering presence? Does it wear a particular outfit that reflects its negative energy? Try to visualize it as vividly as possible, including facial expressions, posture, and gestures. Giving your inner critic a physical form helps create emotional distance from it, making it easier to challenge and confront.

2. Create the Persona of Your Critic: Once you've personified your inner critic in your mind, the next step is to bring it into the physical world. You can draw, sculpt, or even collage your critic—whatever medium feels most comfortable to you. Giving your critic a concrete form allows you to externalize it, making it something you can observe and interact with rather than a force that controls you.

If you choose to draw your critic, start by sketching its basic shape. Pay attention to the details that reflect its critical nature. Perhaps it has exaggerated features—a furrowed brow, a disapproving frown, or crossed arms that signify resistance. Add colors that represent the emotions your critic evokes: dark, heavy tones like gray or black might symbolize negativity, while sharp, jagged lines could reflect its harshness.

Consider using clay, paper, or any other material if you prefer a three-dimensional creation. Mold the figure of your critic, emphasizing the traits you associate with its negative voice. Is it a towering, intimidating figure or a small, sneaky one? What textures reflect its influence—rough, coarse surfaces or smooth but cold materials? Add objects or symbols that enhance its persona, such as chains to represent how it holds you back or thorns to signify the pain it causes.

Creating this figure or image gives you a visual representation of the critic's presence. It separates the critic from your core identity, giving you more control over how you respond to it.

3. Interact with Your Critic: Now that you've given your inner critic a form, it's time to interact purposefully and constructively. Set your creation before you—a drawing, sculpture, or another medium—and take a few moments to observe it. What does it say to you? What phrases or criticisms does it repeat? Write these down if needed so you can fully confront and analyze them.

This stage of the exercise is about taking control of the conversation. You've lived with this voice influencing your thoughts for years, but now you can take charge. Respond to your critic's statements. If it says, "You'll never be good enough," counter with, "I've proven myself capable before, and I can do it again." If it insists, "You always fail," remind it of the times you've succeeded and challenge the absolute nature of its claims.

Next, change the power dynamic by using humor or exaggeration. Turn the critic's harsh words into something so extreme that they lose their sting. For example, if your critic tells you, "You'll never get anything right," respond with a humorous exaggeration, such as, "Oh, so you mean I can't even make a sandwich without messing it up?" The point is to remove the critic's authority by making it sound absurd or exaggerated. This lighthearted approach allows you to emotionally detach from its negativity, making it harder for the critic to affect you.

Finally, speak directly to your inner critic. Tell it that while it may have been trying to protect you in some way—perhaps by encouraging caution or self-preservation—its methods are no longer effective or welcome. Acknowledge its presence but assert that you now choose to lead your life with positivity and empowerment. You can say, "I understand you've been here to keep me from getting hurt, but I don't need you to be so harsh. I have the strength to navigate challenges on my terms."

4. Free Yourself from the Critic's Authority: The goal of this exercise is not to eliminate the inner critic. It's an aspect of your mind that, in some cases, might have once served a purpose. Maybe it helped you stay cautious, avoid risky situations, or be mindful of potential pitfalls. However, the critic's role has likely become too dominant, overshadowing your growth and self-worth. This process aims to reduce the critic's influence and reclaim your inner dialogue for yourself.

To symbolize this power shift, consider performing a ritual of release. If you create a sculpture, you can either keep it as a reminder of your newfound control or disassemble it as an act of liberation. If you drew your critic, you might alter the drawing—perhaps by adding bright colors or positive affirmations around it, representing your new, healthier mindset. Alternatively, you could cross out the negative words or even tear up the drawing, symbolizing your decision to reject the critic's control.

If you're comfortable with it, you could even burn the drawing or sculpture (safely), symbolizing a complete release of the critic's influence over you. The point is to make the act physical and intentional, reinforcing the emotional and psychological liberation you aim for.

Once this symbolic act is complete, take a moment to reflect on how you feel. You may experience a sense of lightness, relief, or empowerment. By confronting your critic, you've taken an essential step in reclaiming your inner dialogue and shaping it into a voice that supports your growth, resilience, and well-being.

Visualization

Freeing yourself from your inner critic

Reflect on how you transformed your critic into a comic character and how you feel now.

Reflection questions

What did your inner critic look like?
What things did it say, and how did it make you feel?
How did it change when you transformed it into something comical?
How do you feel now when you think about that critical voice?

Chapter Five

INTIMATE DIALOGUES

The Deep Connection

Intimate dialogues are profound, meaningful conversations we share with the people who know us best—partners, close friends, children, mentors, and family members. These conversations go far beyond casual exchanges; they are soul-enriching dialogues that offer comfort, growth, and understanding. Through intimate dialogue, we expose our vulnerabilities, confront our fears, and explore our dreams. These moments shape our relationships and define our connections with those we love.

In this chapter, we'll explore the characteristics that define intimate dialogues, the importance of these deep connections, and how we can nurture them to foster emotional growth, personal well-being, and enduring relationships.

At the heart of intimate dialogues is a combination of transparency, honesty, and emotional resonance. Unlike everyday conversations that often skim the surface of life's details, intimate dialogues go deeper, addressing the core of our emotions and inner thoughts. They invite a sense of vulnerability where both participants can express their true selves without fear of judgment. This transparency, where pretense is left behind, creates a safe space for genuine connection.

Empathy plays a central role in these conversations. By actively listening to the other person, engaging fully in their words, and striving to understand their perspective, both parties build a bond that transcends mere social interaction. This shared emotional experience—whether it involves joy, sadness, love, or even conflict—strengthens the connection between the individuals involved.

The Nature of the Connection

As you reflect on these ideas, memories of meaningful conversations with loved ones may come to mind—whether you were sharing a laugh, a heartfelt cry, or simply sitting together in quiet companionship. These are the hallmarks of intimate dialogues: moments of deep exchange that allow us to explore ourselves and our relationships more fully. These long, heartfelt conversations help unveil our inner contradictions, hopes, and fears, all while offering mutual support and growth.

Authenticity takes precedence in intimate dialogues. In these conversations, we can be our most authentic selves, unfiltered and unguarded. Authenticity, however, comes with a challenge: the need to relinquish judgment and the urge to hide behind pretenses. In this type of exchange, taking responsibility for our actions, showing compassion, and fostering mutual respect are essential for establishing and maintaining true intimacy.

These dialogues are more than just conversations—they are spaces of emotional purification and growth. They offer an opportunity for both individuals to confront negative emotions, express pain, and reveal vulnerability. In doing so, a deeper bond is forged, allowing for emotional healing and personal development. However, cultivating such dialogues requires intentional effort, especially in our modern world, where virtual connections often replace face-to-face interaction.

Active Listening: To truly engage in an intimate dialogue, one must practice active listening. This goes beyond merely hearing the words spoken. Active listening involves giving full attention to the other person, reading their body language, maintaining eye contact, and offering verbal and non-verbal responses that show genuine interest. It also means being present in the moment and avoiding distractions that can prevent you from connecting on a deeper level.

Active listening is a gateway to understanding the other person's emotions and needs. By focusing entirely on what is being said—and what is left unsaid—you create an atmosphere of safety and respect. This form of listening also fosters patience and empathy, encouraging both parties to express themselves more openly and honestly. In these intimate dialogues, the listener's role is as crucial as the speaker's, as both must be engaged to flourish.

Ask Open-Ended Questions: Another essential element is asking open-ended questions. Simple inquiries like, "How did that experience impact you?" or "What are your thoughts on this?" can invite the other person to share more of their feelings and insights. These questions foster deeper conversations, allowing both individuals to explore uncharted emotional and intellectual territories. Instead of leading to short answers, these questions create room for reflection and exploration, strengthening the dialogue and deepening the connection between the participants.

Open-ended questions are powerful tools for fostering curiosity and growth within intimate dialogues. They encourage the speaker to delve deeper into their thoughts and feelings, revealing layers of their experience that might otherwise remain hidden. As the conversation unfolds, both participants better understand each other's emotional landscape, creating a more profound and lasting bond.

Share Vulnerabilities: Intimacy also involves sharing one's vulnerabilities, which is closely linked to trust and transparency. Revealing your personal fears, struggles, and emotions builds confidence and encourages the other person to reciprocate, leading to a stronger, more open connection. This sharing fosters an environment where both parties feel seen and heard, knowing their feelings are acknowledged and respected.

Vulnerability is a bridge that connects people on a deeper level. When you allow yourself to be vulnerable in a conversation, you invite the other person into your inner world, offering them a glimpse of your true self. This openness fosters trust, and when both parties share their vulnerabilities, the dialogue becomes a safe space for emotional exploration and mutual support.

Dedicate Time: Time plays a crucial role in fostering intimacy. Quality over quantity is vital. In our hectic lives, it's easy to neglect these moments of connection, but it is essential to prioritize time for deep conversations. Whether through a weekly catch-up session or a spontaneous heart-to-heart, making time for intimate dialogue ensures the ongoing development of meaningful relationships.

In a world where time is often scarce, dedicating time to connect with loved ones signals that they are valued. This intentional investment in the relationship helps build trust and keeps the bond strong. It also creates opportunities for growth and deeper understanding, ensuring the connection remains dynamic and resilient.

Benefits of Intimate Dialogues

Beyond deepening personal bonds, intimate dialogues provide various psychological and emotional benefits. Engaging in these conversations helps reduce feelings of loneliness and isolation. Knowing that someone understands, supports, and listens to you can be reassuring. Furthermore, being valued and seen by someone close to you boosts self-esteem, affirming your sense of identity and self-worth.

Sharing struggles in a supportive environment facilitates emotional healing, as empathy and understanding from another person can be incredibly therapeutic. Validating your feelings by someone you trust helps release pent-up emotions, offering relief and healing. This sense of emotional safety promotes well-being, allowing you to move through life's challenges more resiliently.

Building Emotional Resilience Through Intimate Dialogues: Intimate dialogues also build emotional resilience. A reliable support system allows us to face challenges with greater confidence and strength. When you know someone is there for you—navigating a crisis or celebrating a personal success—you are better equipped to manage stress and adversity.

These deep connections serve as emotional anchors, offering a sense of security and stability during times of uncertainty. Sharing joys and hardships creates a reservoir of emotional strength that can be drawn upon when needed. Intimate dialogues remind us that we are not alone and that support is always available, helping us build resilience and navigate life's ups and downs more easily.

The Power of Shared Activities in Fostering Dialogue: Shared activities, such as preparing meals, walking, or hiking, can also enhance these intimate dialogues. These activities provide a relaxed atmosphere for conversation, allowing dialogue to flow naturally while engaging in a joint task. Whether cooking together, working on a creative project, or walking through nature, these moments create a comfortable setting for meaningful conversation.

Engaging in artistic activities, like painting, drawing, or crafting, stimulates creativity and can provide a unique backdrop for intimate dialogues. For example, creating art together can evoke a sense of flow, where the conversation seamlessly integrates with the creative process, allowing for greater emotional expression and connection. Similarly, reading a book together and discussing it can introduce new topics of conversation, offering fresh insights into each other's thoughts and perspectives.

Intimate Dialogues and Children: Intimate dialogues are not confined to adult relationships. They are also essential in interactions with children. Engaging in intimate conversations with children fosters their emotional intelligence, self-esteem, and sense of security. When we listen attentively to children, validate their emotions, and ask thoughtful questions, we strengthen our bond and help them develop vital skills for understanding and expressing their feelings.

Children who experience these deep connections grow up feeling valued and confident in their communication ability. They learn the importance of expressing their feelings and listening to others, skills that will serve them well. Creating spaces for intimate dialogue with children also ensures they feel supported and understood, reinforcing their emotional well-being and helping them build healthy relationships as they grow.

Key Practices for Intimate Dialogues

Creating and nurturing deep connections through intimate dialogue requires several key practices. Here are a few principles to keep in mind.

Transparency and Authenticity: Strive to be transparent in every conversation. Honesty fosters trust, and authenticity deepens your connection with others.

Active Listening: Give the other person your undivided attention, showing through verbal and non-verbal cues that you are engaged in the conversation.

Ask Open-Ended Questions: Encourage deeper conversations by asking questions that invite reflection and sharing. Avoid yes/no questions and focus on exploring thoughts and emotions.

Share Vulnerabilities: Be open about your experiences, feelings, and fears. Vulnerability creates space for mutual openness and builds trust.

Validate Emotions: Acknowledge the other person's feelings without judgment. Validating emotions creates a safe space for sharing and promotes deeper connection.

Embrace Empathy: Strive to understand the other person's experience from their perspective. Empathy fosters emotional resonance and strengthens bonds.

Respect Boundaries: Trust is built on respecting emotional and personal boundaries. Don't force disclosures or push others into sharing more than they are comfortable with.

Honor Trust and Intimacy: Intimacy cannot exist without trust. Safeguard what is shared during these dialogues and honor the confidentiality of the conversation.

Avoid Judgment: Intimate dialogues thrive in an environment free of judgment. Provide a space for both parties to express themselves without fear of criticism.

When practiced consistently, these guiding principles will help you cultivate more meaningful and intimate dialogues in your relationships, whether with a partner, friend, child, or family member.

Honor the Presence

Building meaningful connections through intimate dialogues requires more than just surface-level conversations; it involves honoring the presence of those who have significantly impacted your life. Whether they are family members, friends, mentors, or colleagues, these individuals have helped shape your journey, offering guidance, support, and companionship during critical moments. Recognizing and celebrating these connections strengthens your relationships and deepens your emotional resilience.

The following exercise is designed to help you reconnect with these individuals, show gratitude for their role in your life, and foster deeper connections in the present. It invites you to reflect on meaningful relationships, express appreciation, and renew the bonds that continue to shape your life.

1. Identify Your Memorable People: Begin by reflecting on the people who have left a lasting, positive impact on your life. These are the individuals who, at crucial moments, supported or inspired you, or perhaps offered their presence when you needed it most. Write down a list of 3-5 names, noting how each person has contributed to your personal growth or emotional well-being. This reflection allows you to bring the value of these intimate connections to the forefront.

For example, you might recall how a mentor guided you through a challenging career decision, or how a close friend provided comfort and encouragement during a difficult personal experience. These moments of reflection help you see the significance of these relationships and remind you of the importance of nurturing them in the present.

2. Prepare the Contact: Next, prepare to reach out to these individuals with intention. This is not just a casual catch-up; it's a moment to express gratitude for the relationship and revisit the connection on a deeper level. You might arrange to meet in person, have a meaningful phone conversation, or send a heartfelt letter or message.

Before reaching out, craft a thoughtful message. Express appreciation for their specific role in your life, recalling a shared memory or a particular quality you admire in them. Be sincere and specific in your gratitude, as this acknowledgment helps reignite the connection. For example, you could say, "I've been reflecting on the past and realized how much your advice helped me through a challenging time. I'm incredibly grateful for your support, and I'd love to reconnect and hear how things are going for both of us now."

This gesture of gratitude is not only an act of kindness but also a way to strengthen the bond between you. It's a reminder that meaningful connections are built on mutual respect, appreciation, and the willingness to be present for one another.

3. Recapture the Vibe of the Meeting: Once you have your message prepared, decide how you will reconnect. If possible, aim for a face-to-face meeting, as this offers the most profound opportunity for meaningful exchange. However, if distance or circumstances make this difficult, a video chat or phone call can still provide a rich, intimate moment of reconnection.

During your conversation, share your message of gratitude and allow the dialogue to unfold naturally. Listen deeply to their stories and experiences, and share your updates with sincerity. These moments of reconnection will remind both of you of the deep bond you share and the importance of nurturing these relationships in the present. By honoring the presence of these people in your life, you cultivate an environment of mutual appreciation and emotional depth.

4. Renew Your Daily Scenes: After you've reconnected, take time to reflect on the experience. How did it feel to rekindle the relationship? What emotions arose during the conversation? How did the exchange strengthen your bond with this person? Write down these reflections in a journal, capturing the key moments and insights from your interaction.

This practice helps solidify the reconnection and provides a space for you to express your thoughts and feelings. It also serves as a reminder that meaningful connections require ongoing effort. Consider making these moments of gratitude and reconnection a regular part of your life, ensuring that you continue to nurture the essential relationships that support your emotional and psychological well-being. Just as plants need consistent care to thrive, so do your relationships.

In intimate dialogues, words hold immense power. They are not just sounds or symbols; they reflect who we are at our core. Through words, we communicate our deepest emotions, promises, and intentions. But beyond the words themselves, the commitment behind them gives them meaning and value. The consistency between what we say and do forms the foundation of any meaningful relationship.

There was a time when words were binding. A simple promise carried weight, without the need for contracts, signatures, or legal guarantees. Trust in someone's word was a testament to their character. If someone said they would be there, they were counted on to follow through—no matter the circumstances. This level of commitment was a social contract, a reflection of integrity and reliability.

To truly honor the words we share in intimate dialogues, we must ensure that our actions align with our promises. Commitment in an intimate relationship means showing up consistently—not only when it's convenient but when it's most important. It means being emotionally available, supportive, and reliable, even when life's demands make it challenging. Without this alignment, words lose their meaning, and relationships begin to fracture.

Chapter Six

Social Dialogues

Livelihoods and Coexistence

Social dialogues are the everyday conversations we have with colleagues, family, neighbors, and friends. These dialogues range from casual, brief exchanges to more in-depth, extended conversations. They connect us to other perspectives and life experiences, offering support and guidance in various situations. In this chapter, you will delve into the characteristics of social dialogues, their importance in community life, and how to improve the quality of these conversations to foster meaningful connections.

Social dialogues occur in a variety of contexts and vary in depth and duration. They are essential for connecting us with others, providing different perspectives and experiences. These dialogues help us navigate our social environments, offering both practical advice and emotional support.

Informal conversations, such as those with co-workers or passing neighbors, often serve to maintain social ties and create a sense of community. These interactions may include casual exchanges about the weather, weekend plans, or current events. Despite their seemingly trivial nature, these conversations play a crucial role in fostering a sense of belonging and mutual respect.

On the other hand, deeper and more extended dialogues with family members or gatherings of friends allow for more meaningful connections and understanding. These conversations often delve into personal experiences, challenges, and aspirations, offering a space to share wisdom, provide support, and reflect on the complexities of life.

Social dialogues are essential for building and maintaining connections. They offer numerous benefits that contribute to our overall well-being and sense of community. Through these dialogues, we develop empathy, understanding, and trust—elements essential to healthy relationships.

The Biology of Socialization

The need for socialization in humans is not merely a matter of entertainment or politeness but a biological function deeply rooted in our evolution as mammals. Like other mammals, humans are born into a state of helplessness, depending on others for survival. Mammals, unlike many other species, have a prolonged period of development in which they need care, protection, and teaching from their parents or community. This dependence creates the basis for a complex network of socialization, where interactions between individuals not only ensure survival but are fundamental to bonding, group cohesion, and the development of individual and collective identity.

In the animal kingdom, mammals display various forms of socialization. For example, wolves engage in cooperative hunting rituals that require constant communication and coordination. Elephants, known for their complex family structures, demonstrate mourning rituals when one of their own dies, evidencing deep emotional bonds. Primates, our closest relatives, use grooming as a social ritual to strengthen bonds and reduce tensions within the group. These behaviors show that socialization is a biological necessity for group cohesion and the functioning of mammalian societies.

Humans, however, are the mammals that require the most support throughout life. From birth, we depend on adults for survival and social learning. Beyond childhood, socialization continues to play a crucial role in our adult lives, not only for physical survival but also for psychological and emotional well-being. Language, unique in its complexity among humans, plays a central role in this process. Through words, we construct a symbolic environment that allows us to communicate ideas, feelings, and experiences, reinforcing our sense of belonging to a group.

The sense of belonging is one of the pillars of human identity. As Daniel Goleman argues in his concept of social intelligence, humans have a social "radar" that allows us to read emotions, anticipate reactions, and adjust our behavior to maintain harmony in interactions. This ability has been crucial to our survival as a species. Humans, though not the strongest or fastest animals, have developed the ability to cooperate, share knowledge, and generate deep emotional bonds. Goleman highlights how our brains connect during social interactions, forming a social circuit in which emotions and thoughts flow between people, creating emotional and physical support networks.

Neuroscientists Antonio Damasio and Lisa Barrett have further explored the role of emotions in human socialization. Damasio emphasizes that emotions are complex responses involving both body and mind, playing a key role in decision-making and social relationships. Barrett posits that emotions are constructed through our interactions with the social environment and shaped by the language and culture we are immersed in. This highlights the importance of words not only as tools of communication but as elements that shape our emotions, identities, and social connections.

Through social interactions, we reinforce our commonalities while also defining what makes us unique. Maintaining social dialogues is not just an obligation or pastime but an ancestral necessity that ensures group cohesion and the emotional well-being of its members.

Social Connection

Emotions play a fundamental role in human communication, motivating behavior and giving deep meaning to life. Our ability to experience a wide range of emotions—joy, love, interest, anger—enriches our personal, social, and professional lives. Emotions are woven into every human experience, shaping how we interact with the world.

Social dialogues are vital for fostering empathy and understanding. Engaging in these dialogues allows us to appreciate others' perspectives, reducing misunderstandings and conflicts. They create a support network, offering reassurance and comfort when needed. These conversations foster a sense of belonging, helping us feel connected to the larger social group.

Sharing diverse perspectives through social dialogues also promotes personal growth. Conversations challenge our assumptions, encourage critical thinking, and broaden our horizons. For example, an informal chat with a colleague about their family may provide fascinating insights into different traditions and values. Hearing how someone overcame a personal challenge or achieved a goal can inspire and motivate us.

Social dialogues also offer support and guidance. Whether we face a personal challenge or seek advice, conversations provide valuable resources. Discussing a difficult situation with a trusted colleague or neighbor might offer key insights or help alleviate stress.

Nurturing Meaningful Affective Dialogues

It is essential to focus on the quality of these conversations to maximize the benefits of social and affective dialogues. The depth and richness of our social interactions directly affect our relationships' quality and overall well-being. Here are some key strategies to improve the quality of dialogues.

Be Present: Show genuine interest in the conversation by giving your full attention to the other person. Avoid distractions, such as checking your phone or thinking about different tasks, and focus on actively listening to what they are saying. This demonstrates that you value their perspective and creates a space for meaningful exchange.

Ask Thoughtful Questions: Encourage deeper conversations by asking open-ended questions that invite the other person to share their thoughts and experiences. Questions like, "What inspired you to pursue that path?" or "How do you feel about that situation?" can lead to more insightful and engaging dialogues.

Share Personal Experiences: Being open about your experiences fosters a sense of connection and encourages others to do the same. Sharing stories about your challenges, successes, or reflections can create a reciprocal exchange that deepens the conversation.

Listen Actively: Active listening involves more than just hearing spoken words. It requires paying attention to the speaker's body language, tone of voice, and emotions. Show your engagement by maintaining eye contact, nodding, and offering verbal affirmations. Reflecting on the other person's words can also demonstrate understanding and empathy.

Maintain Empathy: Empathy is the foundation of meaningful affective dialogues. Try to understand the other person's emotions and perspectives, even if they differ from your own. Empathy fosters connection, builds trust, and helps create a supportive and caring environment.

Respect Boundaries and Opinions: Respect the opinions and experiences of others, even if they don't align with your own. Avoid interrupting or dismissing their views, and instead engage in respectful dialogue that honors their perspective. Creating an atmosphere of mutual respect ensures that everyone feels valued and heard.

Overcoming Social Difficulties

Despite the fundamental need for socialization, many people experience anxiety and discomfort in social settings. Social anxiety, the fear of being judged or negatively evaluated, can limit personal and professional development. This anxiety may stem from early experiences, such as a lack of assertiveness or communication skills in family or educational environments.

Low self-esteem is a common psychological factor contributing to social anxiety. Social comparison theory, developed by psychologist Leon Festinger, suggests that when people feel insecure, they compare themselves negatively to others, reinforcing their anxiety. Lack of assertiveness further exacerbates this, making it difficult to express thoughts and feelings confidently.

Social anxiety can lead to avoidance of important interactions, affecting both personal and professional relationships. However, practical approaches—such as active listening, small contributions to conversations, and preparing talking points—can help ease anxiety and build confidence.

Social anxiety is not an insurmountable barrier. By practicing social strategies, developing assertive communication, and seeking support, you can reduce anxiety, engage effectively in group interactions, and build meaningful relationships. Socialization is a fundamental necessity for emotional and psychological well-being. With patience and commitment, you can overcome fears and enjoy the human connections vital to your happiness.

Chapter Seven

DIFFICULT DIALOGUES

Dealing with Negative Emotions

You have probably dreaded a conversation at some point, knowing it would be fraught with tension, misunderstandings, or negative emotions. Has this feeling ever occurred to you? Difficult dialogues are inevitable, whether they arise from disagreements, misunderstandings, or the need to communicate unpleasant information. These conversations can occur in various settings—family, work, or social—and often significantly impact our emotions and mental well-being.

Difficult dialogues aren't just about words exchanged between two people. They carry emotional weight that can influence our relationships, self-esteem, and mental health. However, mastering certain techniques and strategies can transform these difficult moments into growth, understanding, and connection opportunities. The key lies in preparation, emotional regulation, and understanding the conversations you're dealing with.

This chapter will explore different types of difficult conversations, their characteristics, and their effects on your emotional state and relationships. Most importantly, you'll learn to manage these situations calmly and confidently. With the right approach, difficult dialogues can become less daunting and more constructive, whether it's a work negotiation, a family dispute, or communicating unpleasant news.

Types of Difficult Dialogues

Difficult dialogues often trigger a cascade of intense emotions. Anxiety and fear can arise from anticipating a negative outcome. You might fear rejection, conflict, or the emotional strain of confronting someone with bad news. Anger and frustration may surface during the conversation, particularly when you feel misunderstood or attacked. Sadness and disappointment often follow if the conversation doesn't go the way you hoped.

Equally important are the thoughts that accompany these emotions. During difficult conversations, your mind may create a negative spiral, where doubts about your abilities, worthiness, or the potential consequences of the dialogue take over. This mental loop can heighten emotional responses, leading to a cycle where fear feeds into frustration, making it harder to navigate the conversation effectively.

Difficult dialogues come in many forms, each with its unique challenges. Some situations require sensitivity and empathy, while others demand firmness and assertiveness. By categorizing the types of dialogues, you can better prepare yourself for each situation. Below, we will explore some of the most common types.

Negotiations and Conflicts: Negotiations often involve disputes over resources, responsibilities, or values. For example, you might need to negotiate over a project role or budget allocation in the workplace. These conversations require a delicate balance between asserting your needs and empathizing with the other person's position. Without careful handling, these situations can easily escalate into conflicts, especially if both parties are unwilling to compromise.

Imagine negotiating with a colleague over who should take on a particular responsibility. The conversation can quickly become heated if both parties feel strongly about their stance. To avoid this, you must practice active listening, clearly communicate your needs, and be open to finding a middle ground. Sometimes, the intervention of a neutral third party—such as a manager or HR representative—may be necessary to mediate and ensure a fair outcome.

Personal negotiations—such as deciding how to divide household responsibilities with a partner—can also lead to conflict if both parties are not clear about expectations. In these cases, setting boundaries early and maintaining open communication can help prevent minor issues from snowballing into more significant conflicts.

Conversations with Difficult People: Some individuals are naturally more challenging to communicate with. Whether they are confrontational, manipulative, or possess narcissistic tendencies, these individuals can make dialogues especially difficult. Understanding their behavior and maintaining emotional distance is key. For example, when dealing with a manipulative person, it's important to recognize that their tactics—whether they play the victim or try to control the conversation—are designed to throw you off balance.

A typical scenario might involve a family member constantly playing the victim, blaming others for their misfortune. Engaging in a conversation with such a person requires assertiveness. Instead of getting drawn into their emotional manipulation, you must stand your ground and set firm boundaries. For example, saying, "I understand you're upset, but I cannot take responsibility for what's happened," is a way to acknowledge their feelings without being manipulated into guilt.

In work settings, conversations with difficult personalities—such as managers or colleagues who dominate discussions or avoid accountability—require professionalism and clear expectations. You maintain control of the conversation by sticking to your points without intimidation.

Communicating Unpleasant Information: Delivering bad news is never easy, whether in a personal or professional setting. You may need to inform your team about layoffs, tell a friend you can no longer support them financially, or talk to a family member about a severe health issue. These conversations can provoke strong emotional reactions, so approaching them with sensitivity is essential.

In the workplace, providing negative feedback requires clarity. Instead of being vague or cushioning the truth, state the facts clearly and offer constructive criticism. For example, "I've noticed that your recent work hasn't met the deadlines we discussed" is more effective than "It seems like you've been a bit slow lately." At the same time, it's essential to give space for the other person to process the information and respond.

Communicating unpleasant information also extends to difficult personal conversations, such as breaking up with a partner or setting boundaries with a toxic friend. In these cases, you must be prepared for emotional reactions and give the other person time to process the news. Being honest and direct, though challenging, is often the kindest approach in the long run.

Complicated Relationships: Family disputes, unresolved friendship conflicts, and issues within long-standing relationships can lead to some of the most emotionally charged dialogues. These situations often involve years of history, misunderstandings, and emotional baggage, making them particularly challenging to navigate.

For instance, discussing caregiving responsibilities with siblings often brings up unresolved family dynamics. Each person may have different expectations and emotional ties to the issue. Setting a calm, neutral environment for such conversations is essential. Active listening, empathy, and clearly expressing your needs are vital. For example, "I know we all want the best for Mom, but I'm finding it hard to manage everything alone" opens up the conversation without blaming anyone.

Strategies for Managing Difficult Dialogues

Successfully managing difficult dialogues requires preparation, self-awareness, and the proper communication techniques. Let's dive into critical strategies.

Prepare in Advance: Preparation is crucial when facing a difficult conversation. Take time beforehand to think about the key points you want to address and anticipate possible reactions. This doesn't mean rehearsing every word but having a clear idea of what you need to communicate and how you will manage any emotional responses that arise.

For example, if you need to confront a friend about a behavior bothering you, think through the conversation in advance. What are the key issues you want to raise? What's your desired outcome? This preparation helps you stay focused and calm, even if the other person becomes defensive.

Practice with a trusted friend or partner before delivering difficult news or engaging in a challenging conversation. Rehearsing out loud allows you to refine your message, gain confidence, and consider alternative ways to approach sensitive topics.

Emotional Regulation: Managing your own emotions is just as important as managing the conversation itself. Practicing emotional regulation techniques can help you remain calm, even in the most intense dialogues. Deep breathing, mindfulness, or visualization can reduce anxiety and center yourself before and during the conversation.

Before you sit down with a difficult colleague, take a few minutes to breathe deeply and visualize a positive outcome. This will help you keep your emotions in check and stay focused and composed.

Another effective technique is to practice grounding exercises during the conversation. If you feel overwhelmed, pause mentally to focus on your surroundings, your breath, or something physical, such as the sensation of your feet on the ground. This will help you stay anchored in the moment and prevent your emotions from escalating.

Assertiveness: Assertiveness is essential to navigating difficult dialogues. Being assertive means expressing your thoughts and feelings clearly and respectfully. It balances being too passive (where your needs are neglected) and aggressive (where the conversation becomes destructive).

In a family argument about caregiving responsibilities, rather than remaining silent or becoming confrontational, use assertive statements like, "I feel overwhelmed by the current situation and need more support from everyone." This allows you to express your needs without triggering defensiveness in others.

Assertiveness isn't just about standing your ground—it's about creating a respectful space for open communication. It fosters collaboration and mutual respect by allowing both parties to express their perspectives without fear of being attacked or dismissed.

Use "I" Statements: Under challenging dialogues, "I" statements can help reduce defensiveness and focus the conversation on the issue rather than personal attacks. For instance, saying, "I feel frustrated when deadlines are missed," is more effective than "You never meet deadlines." The latter will likely put the other person on the defensive, while the former focuses on your feelings and experience.

"I" statements help convey your feelings without assigning blame. This opens the door for a more constructive conversation and encourages the other person to respond similarly thoughtfully. It keeps the dialogue focused on the issue and helps prevent escalation.

Active Listening: Active listening is one of the most effective ways to defuse tension in a difficult conversation. By showing that you are genuinely listening—maintaining eye contact, nodding, or summarizing what the other person has said—you can make them feel heard, often reducing their defensiveness and opening the door to more productive dialogue.

For example, if your sibling is upset during a family dispute, summarizing their concerns with a statement like, "It sounds like you're worried about the financial burden," shows that you understand their perspective.

Active listening goes beyond simply hearing the other person's words. It involves empathy and understanding, ensuring the other person feels valued and validated in the conversation. This reduces the likelihood of defensive reactions and opens the door to more cooperative problem-solving.

Addressing psychopathic traits

A psychopathic person is, in psychological terms, someone who displays a profound lack of empathy, a natural inclination to manipulate, and a marked desire to control others. Psychopathy is not simply a matter of immoral or antisocial behavior; it is a pathology that affects interpersonal interactions in significant ways. Psychopaths tend to be charming on the surface, which makes them difficult to identify at first. Still, their intentions are often directed toward satisfying their own desires at the expense of others.

Modern psychology has extensively studied these traits and has established that individuals with psychopathic characteristics often show an inability to feel guilt or remorse. The lack of emotional connection with others allows them to act without considering the moral consequences of their actions. Relationships with psychopathic individuals can be emotionally destructive, as they employ tactics such as manipulation, lying, and intimidation to get what they want.

Science has proven that the brains of psychopaths function differently. Neuroscientific studies have shown alterations in brain areas related to emotional regulation and decision-making. Identifying a psychopathic person can be challenging due to their ability to camouflage themselves in society. Psychopaths often present themselves as charismatic and successful individuals, but beneath this facade, their behavior reveals a lack of regard for the feelings and needs of others.

Conversations with these individuals can be tricky. In this framework, let us dedicate some essential aspects to caring for these conversations. These types of personalities require special care. You may have been involved in a manipulative romantic relationship, in a work or business relationship, or have family members with these characteristics.

Establish Boundaries: Establishing and maintaining firm boundaries is essential when conversing with someone you recognize as manipulative. Boundaries are about controlling the conversation and protecting your mental and emotional space. By clearly defining what behavior is acceptable and what isn't, you prevent the other person from gaining control over the dialogue or over you.

One effective boundary-setting technique is to state what you will and will not tolerate. For example, if a manipulative family member tries to guilt-trip you into doing something, you can respond with, "I understand that you're upset, but I'm not going to make decisions based on guilt. Let's discuss the issue at hand without using emotional manipulation."

Maintain Control of the Conversation: In addition to setting boundaries, maintaining conversation control is vital when dealing with manipulative individuals. This doesn't mean dominating the dialogue but ensuring it remains respectful and on topic. If the conversation evolves into personal attacks, deflection, or emotional manipulation, redirect it back to the issue.

For instance, if someone starts to blame you for something unrelated, you can say, "I'd like to focus on the main point right now. We can discuss other concerns at a different time, but we must resolve this issue first." This approach allows you to stay calm and centered while preventing the manipulative person from steering the conversation in a direction that benefits them.

Note When to End the Conversation: Sometimes, despite your best efforts, a manipulative person will refuse to engage in a respectful and productive conversation. In these situations, it's okay to walk away. Ending a toxic discussion is not a sign of defeat; it's a demonstration of self-respect and emotional self-care.

If a conversation becomes repetitive, accusatory, or emotionally draining, you might say, "I don't think this conversation is going anywhere productive right now. Let's take a break and revisit it later if necessary." This preserves your well-being and clearly conveys that you will not engage in unproductive or harmful dialogues.

In extreme cases, mainly when dealing with people who exhibit psychopathic or narcissistic traits, it may be necessary to cut off communication altogether. Psychopaths and narcissists are often expert manipulators who lack empathy and view relationships as a means to an end. If you find yourself constantly drained or emotionally harmed by these interactions, it's essential to protect yourself by limiting contact or even ending the relationship if necessary.

Preserving Your Dignity

Since ancient times, cultures worldwide have practiced creating and using protective objects and items to help them cope with life's uncertainties. These objects, whether amulets, talismans, sacred stones, or engraved symbols, served as tangible tools that connected people to their inner power and reminded them of their strength in times of difficulty. Warriors carried objects of protection before battle, healers used talismans to channel healing energies, and travelers kept amulets to guide their way.

These objects not only provided a sense of physical security but also served as emotional and spiritual anchors. They allowed people to stay connected to their values, ancestors, and earth, reminding them of their purpose and power in any situation. Today, although we live in a modern, technologically advanced world, the underlying principle remains the same: having something to remind us of who we are can be a powerful resource for facing difficult situations with dignity and calm.

The following exercise is intended to help you prepare a dignity preservation kit inspired by the wisdom of ancient cultures that connects you to your inner power and gives you the strength to face any difficult situation.

Preserving dignity in a difficult situation is essential because dignity is the foundation of self-esteem and self-respect. In a conflict or a tense conversation, it is easy to get carried away and act in ways you may later regret. However, maintaining dignity allows you to respond from a place of calm and self-control rather than reacting impulsively. By preserving dignity, you protect your integrity in the face of violent or intimidating situations, set clear boundaries, and show others that you deserve to be treated with respect. This not only strengthens our position in the conversation but can also positively influence the dynamics of the dialogue, promoting a more constructive and respectful exchange. Preserving dignity, therefore, is essential to navigating difficult situations without losing our essence, maintaining our inner peace, and ensuring that our actions and words reflect our deepest values.

1. Prepare the preventive kit: Reflect on the elements that can be anchors of protection and inner strength. These elements will be the core of your preventive kit and help you maintain calm and dignity when circumstances demand it. Write down a list of your most important values that define who you are and how you want to behave in any situation. These values will be the foundation of your dignity and will form a central part of your preventive kit. List the inner qualities that have helped you in difficult situations. They may include patience, listening skills, self-discipline, resilience, or any other quality that allows you to remain calm. Identify external objects or items that can serve as modern talismans: a touchstone, a particular photo, a small symbolic figure, or a piece of clothing that makes you feel safe.

2. Create your preventive kit: With the identified elements in mind, it's time to create your first aid kit, which can be physical or mental, but the important thing is that it is full of resources that you can turn to when you face difficult situations. If you create a physical first aid kit, place some items that remind you of your inner values and resources in a small case. Native Americans called this a "medicine bag." For example, you might include a small card with your values written on it, a stone you can hold to anchor you in the present, or a list of personal affirmations reinforcing your dignity. If you prefer a mental approach, visualize a box, or you can visualize a specially colored bubble in your mind where you keep all the tools and resources you have identified. You can open this mental medicine cabinet or enter the bubble when you feel that a problematic situation is affecting your dignity. Imagine taking out of that box the tools you need at that moment.

3. Rely on your medicine cabinet: The next time you face a difficult situation, turn to your first aid kit. Before you react, take a moment to remember your values, use your inner resources, and, if possible, connect with the symbolic objects in your physical kit. Practice a breathing technique, repeat a personal affirmation, or simply recall a past situation in which you acted with dignity to keep yourself calm. If you carry an object from your medicine cabinet, such as a touchstone or bracelet, hold it or wear it as a physical reminder of your dignity and inner strength. Let it anchor you in the present and remind you of your ability to face the situation calmly.

Visualization

Facing Difficult Dialogues

Reflect on the difficult dialogue you visualized. Describe how you handled the conversation and felt during and after the dialogue.

Reflection questions

What type of difficult dialogue did you visualize?
What emotions came up during the conversation?
How did you feel at the end of the dialogue?

CHAPTER EIGHT

VIRTUAL DIALOGUES

CONVERSATION THROUGH A SCREEN

Social media has become an integral part of our daily lives in today's digital world. It offers a platform to connect, share, and communicate with others across vast distances. However, these virtual conversations come with their own set of challenges. Social networks can be incredibly engaging and, at times, addictive, often interfering with our mental well-being and daily routines. This chapter explores how virtual dialogues impact our emotions and brain functions, helping you maintain a healthier relationship with an environment that is as captivating as potentially addictive.

Virtual dialogues, mediated by an interface—a screen—are unique. Whether we write messages, share videos, or interact through content, the absence of physical presence alters communication dynamics. Body language, facial expressions, and tone of voice—crucial in face-to-face conversations—often disappear or are diminished in virtual dialogues. This absence can result in misinterpretations, emotional disconnects, and conflicts due to a lack of nuance.

Although we often associate virtual interactions with convenience and speed, emotions still play a significant role in these dialogues. While digital spaces might seem detached from real life, the emotions we experience while engaging with others online are very real. The absence of non-verbal cues prompts users to employ emojis, gifs, and punctuation marks as substitutes to convey emotional tones. While helpful, these symbols cannot fully replicate the depth and richness of face-to-face emotional exchanges, often leading to misunderstandings.

Consider how a simple message, devoid of context or tone, might be interpreted differently than intended. For example, a brief "okay" might seem dismissive to the recipient, even if the sender meant it as a neutral or agreeable response. The subtlety of facial expressions or the reassurance of a smile is missing, which can distort how emotions are communicated.

The disconnection between digital communication and emotional interpretation can also amplify negative experiences, such as frustration or anxiety. These misunderstandings often escalate into conflicts that might not have occurred in a face-to-face conversation, where body language would have clarified the true intent.

Types of Virtual Dialogues Across Platforms

Each social media platform fosters different interactions, shaping how we communicate and influencing how we engage with others. Understanding these differences is essential to recognizing how they contribute to positive and negative emotional responses.

Instagram – The Visual Dialogue: Conversations on Instagram revolve around visuals—photos, stories, and videos. Users engage with short comments and "likes," creating a validation loop where approval from others can become an emotional trigger. The platform encourages a filtered version of reality, with users spending hours editing their photos to present their best selves. This constant need for validation often leads to anxiety when posts don't receive the expected number of likes or comments. For example, a person might post an image expecting praise, only to feel disappointment or insecurity when it doesn't garner the anticipated attention. This cycle can result in compulsive checking, a fixation on external validation, and feelings of inadequacy.

X (formerly Twitter) – **The Rapid-Fire Dialogue**: On X, conversations are concise and focus on current events, opinions, and trends. The platform's character limit encourages brevity, leading to rapid-fire exchanges that often escalate into heated debates. X's real-time nature fosters a sense of immediacy, making it a go-to source for news and personal opinions. However, the urge to constantly check for updates can become addictive, pulling users into endless cycles of scrolling and engagement. The brevity of posts can also strip conversations of nuance. Complex issues are reduced to bite-sized arguments, often missing important context, leading to misunderstandings or aggressive exchanges. This environment, while dynamic, can create emotional exhaustion as users engage in frequent, often combative, dialogues.

Facebook – The Lengthy Exchange: Facebook supports more extensive conversations, from personal updates to group discussions and shared content. It offers space for deeper connections but can also expose users to a wide range of positive and negative content. The platform often draws users into lengthy discussions or endless scrolling, which can detract from productivity and leave them emotionally drained. In many cases, Facebook users become involved in heated debates within comment sections, particularly when discussing sensitive topics like politics or social issues. The lack of face-to-face interaction can encourage some users to express themselves more harshly than they would in person, leading to confrontations and emotional distress.

WhatsApp – The Instant Dialogue: WhatsApp is a platform for private, instant communication, much like traditional text messaging but with added functionalities like group chats, voice messaging, and multimedia sharing. While intimate and immediate, these conversations can lead to compulsive checking, especially in group settings where constant notifications demand attention. Work-related conversations on WhatsApp often blur the lines between personal time and professional obligations. Employees might feel pressured to respond to messages outside of work hours, contributing to burnout and a sense of being perpetually "on call." The ease of access to private messaging can make it difficult to disengage from ongoing conversations, even when they become overwhelming.

TikTok – The Creative Dialogue: TikTok's short-form video content offers a platform for creativity, entertainment, and self-expression. However, its fast-paced nature, driven by an algorithm that tailors content to user preferences, makes it highly addictive. Users can easily lose track of time while consuming personalized content that appeals to their interests. The platform's emphasis on likes and views can also drive feelings of competition and anxiety among younger users. They may feel pressured to maintain popularity or achieve viral success, contributing to emotional stress if their content doesn't perform as expected. The addictive nature of TikTok's infinite scrolling feature can also encourage prolonged use, affecting attention spans and cognitive focus.

The Impact on Mental Health

While social media platforms provide opportunities for connection and expression, they also pose risks to mental health. One of the most prominent effects is the pressure to seek validation through likes, comments, and shares. This creates a cycle of dependency on external approval, where self-worth becomes tied to online engagement.

For example, many users experience FOMO (Fear of Missing Out) when they see friends attending events or engaging in activities they're not part of.

This fear can lead to anxiety and insecurity as people feel left out or believe they are not living up to the idealized lives portrayed on social media.

Several studies have shown that social media addiction stems from the brain's need for connection and validation. Platforms like Instagram and TikTok are designed to exploit these desires by offering instant gratification through notifications, likes, and comments. Features like endless scrolling and algorithm-driven content keep users hooked, similar to the way gambling machines offer intermittent rewards.

The unpredictability of these rewards makes social media highly addictive. Users never know when they'll receive a new like or comment, encouraging them to check their phones repeatedly throughout the day. This behavior can mirror that of other addictive activities, creating a dependency on digital interactions.

Excessive use of social media doesn't just affect mental health—it can have physical consequences as well. Prolonged screen time can lead to eyestrain, disrupted sleep patterns due to blue light exposure, and poor posture from hunching over phones and laptops.

Additionally, using emojis, gifs, and shorthand language on social media platforms can hinder cognitive development, particularly among younger users. Relying on these abbreviated forms of communication may limit language skills and reduce the ability to engage in complex, meaningful conversations. Over time, this could impact social interactions and emotional intelligence.

While social media is a powerful tool for connection, it's essential to engage with it mindfully. Setting boundaries—such as limiting screen time, turning off notifications, or taking regular breaks—can help mitigate the negative effects of constant engagement. It's also important to be aware of your emotional responses while using social media. If you feel anxious, frustrated, or inadequate, take a step back and reflect on how virtual interactions affect your mental well-being.

You can navigate virtual dialogues with greater control and clarity by being more conscious of how social media influences your emotions, behaviors, and physical health. The goal is to enjoy the benefits of these platforms without falling into the trap of addiction, emotional dependency, or burnout.

Living with Virtuality

To evaluate your participation in virtual dialogues, take the following test. This 10-question test, with three rating scales, will help you understand your level of rapport with virtual communication and provide suggestions based on your score.

1 - How often do you check for messages or notifications on your phone or computer?
a) Rarely
b) Sometimes
c) Frequently

2 - Are you anxious or upset if you can't access your phone or the Internet?
a) Not at all
b) From time to time
c) Very much

3 - How much time do you spend a day on social networks?
a) Less than 1 hour
b) 1-3 hours
c) More than 3 hours

4 - Do you frequently participate in online discussions or debates?
a) Rarely

b) Occasionally

c) Frequently

5 - How often do you share personal information on social networks?

a) Rarely

b) Sometimes

c) Frequently

6 - Do you use the telephone or computer during meals or social gatherings?

a) Rarely

b) Occasionally

c) Frequently

7 - How often do you need to look at your phone or computer as soon as you get up?

a) Rarely

b) Sometimes

c) Frequently

8 - Do you lose track of time while surfing the Internet or social networks?

a) Rarely

b) Occasionally

c) Frequently

9 - How often do you feel compelled to respond immediately to messages or notifications?

a) Rarely

b) Sometimes

c) Frequently

10 - Do you struggle to concentrate on tasks without looking at your phone or computer?
a) Rarely
b) Occasionally
c) Frequently

Assign the following score to your answers
a = 1 point
b = 2 points
c = 3 points

Evaluation Scales
10-16 points: **Healthy engagement with virtual dialogues.** You have a balanced approach to virtual communication. Continue to maintain this balance and notice any changes in your habits.

17-23 points: **Moderate dependence on virtual dialogues.** You spend significant time on virtual dialogues, which can affect your daily life. Consider setting limits, such as designated screen-free times, to reduce dependence.

24-30 points: **High dependence on virtual dialogues.** Your virtual dialogues may negatively affect your life. Setting stricter boundaries, taking regular breaks, and engaging in offline activities can help mitigate this dependency.

Take Care of Your Virtual Dialogues

In a world dominated by screens, it is crucial to establish boundaries that help us maintain a balanced relationship with technology. Whether through social media, messaging apps, or other digital platforms, virtual dialogues have become integral to our daily interactions. However, these conversations can take over without careful management, leaving us overwhelmed, distracted, and disconnected from the real world. To keep our virtual dialogues from dominating our lives, we must develop strategies to manage our time online and preserve our mental well-being.

Let's take a moment to explore practical ways you can incorporate healthy habits into your life to prevent virtual dialogues from taking control and ensure they enhance rather than detract from your overall well-being.

Set Clear Boundaries: One of the most effective ways to protect your mental space is to set specific times to check your phone or social media. Constant engagement with digital devices, especially during meals, family gatherings, or social events, detracts from meaningful, in-person interactions and fosters a habit of distraction. To combat this, focus on being fully present in the moment. When you are present with the people around you, your relationships strengthen, and you prevent the anxiety that arises from needing to be constantly "on" in the digital world.

For instance, make it a habit to check your messages only during specific times, such as in the morning and evening, rather than constantly throughout the day. This intentional approach can drastically reduce the compulsion to continually check for notifications, freeing your mind from the digital tug-of-war that often distracts us from what truly matters. You can take back your time and mental clarity by controlling when and how you engage with your phone or social media.

Schedule Digital Detoxes: Plan regular breaks from your devices—digital detoxes don't have to be extreme, but they should be intentional. Start small by allocating a few hours a day, or one full day each week, to be entirely screen-free. Use this time to reconnect with offline hobbies, engage in outdoor activities, or spend quality time with loved ones. These breaks give your mind the necessary space to rest from digital platforms' constant influx of information. They also allow you to reset your focus, reminding you that life outside the screen is rich with opportunities for fulfillment.

You may find that stepping away from screens, even for short periods, brings a sense of clarity and a renewed purpose to your interactions. The more you practice digital detox, the more you will appreciate the mental peace that comes from creating a healthy separation between your digital and real-life engagements.

Engage in Offline Hobbies: One of the simplest yet most effective ways to counterbalance excessive screen time is to rediscover offline activities. Hobbies such as reading, painting, writing, hiking, or gardening offer you the chance to reconnect with the physical world. These activities provide a much-needed break from virtual distractions and help reduce the stress and anxiety digital overload brings.

For example, if you enjoy painting or creating art, you might find that time spent in creative expression helps calm your mind and refocus your energy. When you immerse yourself in a physical activity that demands your full attention, the urge to check your phone or scroll through social media fades. Over time, these offline hobbies become a source of mental relief and personal fulfillment, offering a refreshing sense of freedom from the digital world.

Use Technology to Control It: Instead of letting technology control you, use it to your advantage by employing tools that monitor and regulate your usage. Apps that track screen time or allow you to set limits on certain platforms are excellent tools for building awareness about your digital habits. By seeing how much time you spend on social media, you may feel motivated to make conscious adjustments.

For example, set daily limits for specific apps or use features like "Do Not Disturb" during work hours or meals to create a more mindful and controlled relationship with your devices. You could also use technology to set reminders that encourage breaks from screens. Using these tools, you regain control over your digital habits and establish a more balanced, intentional way of engaging with technology.

Create Technology-Free Zones: Designating specific areas of your home as technology-free zones can help reduce the compulsion to check your phone or tablet. For example, consider making your dining room, living room, or bedroom a space free of phones or other devices. This encourages more meaningful interactions with others and reinforces the idea that technology should not dominate every aspect of your life.

Creating spaces where screens aren't allowed encourages a healthier relationship with your surroundings and the people around you. You'll find that meals, conversations, and rest become more fulfilling when they are free from the distractions of digital notifications and social media updates. These technology-free zones allow you to cultivate deeper connections with your loved ones and with your thoughts, promoting a sense of balance between the virtual and physical worlds.

Reflect on Online Interactions: After engaging in online conversations, whether through messaging apps or social media, take a moment to reflect on how those interactions made you feel. Were they enriching and uplifting, or did they leave you feeling anxious, drained, or disconnected? If certain platforms or people consistently bring negativity into your life, consider limiting your engagement with them.

Being mindful of how virtual dialogues affect your emotional state can help you make better choices about where and with whom you spend your digital time. Protect your mental health by stepping back from toxic interactions and focusing on those that bring positivity, inspiration, or learning. You can create a virtual space that aligns with your values and emotional well-being by consciously curating your online interactions.

Prioritize Face-to-Face Interactions: Whenever possible, prioritize in-person conversations over virtual ones. Face-to-face interactions provide a deeper connection and emotional satisfaction that online exchanges often lack. By seeking out more in-person interactions, you can strengthen your relationships and experience the emotional rewards of authentic human connection.

These interactions don't have to be grand gestures—simple activities like meeting a friend for coffee instead of texting can significantly affect how connected and fulfilled you feel. Human beings are wired for real-world interaction, and nurturing those in-person connections can bring depth and joy that is difficult to replicate online.

Educate Yourself About Privacy: In today's online world, privacy is more important than ever. Understanding how to protect your personal information can give you peace of mind and empower you to navigate virtual spaces more confidently. Take the time to review the privacy settings on your devices and social media platforms regularly. Adjust these settings to ensure you only share the information you are comfortable making public.

Being conscious of your digital footprint helps safeguard your personal information and reduces the risk of oversharing. By protecting your privacy, you maintain control over your online presence and reduce the potential for unwanted intrusion into your personal life.

A Deal With Your Phone

In today's world, where our phones have become constant companions, we must establish healthier boundaries. A relationship with technology requires balance, where we are in control rather than allowing our devices to dominate our lives. In the following exercise, you will engage in a creative, intimate dialogue with your phone. This exercise is designed to help you redefine your relationship with your phone and virtual assistant, making technology a positive force in your life rather than a source of stress.

1. Prepare the Conversation: First, find a quiet place to be alone with your phone. Imagine that your phone is a close friend with whom you are about to have an honest conversation. Hold your phone in your hand or place it on a table. As you begin this imaginative dialogue, reflect on the essential things you need from your phone.

Do you rely on your phone for connection with loved ones, quick access to information, or entertainment? Write down these positive contributions your phone makes to your life. You can also include your virtual assistant (Siri, Alexa, Google Assistant, etc.) in the conversation, acknowledging how they contribute to your day-to-day activities.

2. Define the Boundaries of Your Deal: It's time to establish boundaries with your phone and virtual assistant. Ask questions as if you were having a real conversation:

How can I use you in a way that enriches my life without consuming it?

How can we ensure that my conversations through you are respectful and safe?

What boundaries do I need to set so our time together doesn't become a source of stress or anxiety?

How can I protect my privacy while enjoying your benefits?

What signs should I watch for to know when it's time to disconnect?

Reflect on these questions and consider how your phone or virtual assistant might respond. What boundaries do you need to establish to maintain a healthy relationship?

3. Create a Coexistence Agreement: Finally, write down a "contract" or agreement you commit to following in your relationship with your phone. This could include limiting the use of certain apps, setting specific times to check messages, or making your bedroom a phone-free zone. Creating clear rules will help ensure your technology usage remains balanced and healthy.

While imaginative, this exercise allows you to redefine your relationship with technology consciously. By setting boundaries and reflecting on "what do I need from you?" you establish a healthier, more mindful dynamic that benefits your well-being.

Chapter Nine

TOXIC NARRATIVES

The Structure of the Traps

Narratives are symbolic structures that shape our interpretations and experiences. They are the stories we tell ourselves—often unconsciously—that influence our emotions, behaviors, and perceptions of the world. While positive and constructive narratives can foster personal growth, resilience, and well-being, toxic narratives can trap us in cycles of negative thinking, reinforcing unproductive habits and limiting beliefs.

In this chapter, we will explore the characteristics of toxic narratives, how they infiltrate our thoughts, and how they shape our reality. You'll discover how toxic narratives affect your emotions and behavior through the power of language and how to apply practical tools to transform these toxic thought patterns into empowering internal dialogues.

Recognizing Toxic Narratives

Toxic narratives are often persistent and deeply ingrained, which makes them particularly dangerous. These negative internal stories are more than just fleeting thoughts; they are recurring beliefs and patterns that shape how you interpret your life and interact with the world. They often reinforce feelings of helplessness, fear, or frustration, leaving you stuck in unproductive behaviors.

One key characteristic of toxic narratives is that they are frequently based on negative self-talk. This can manifest as questions or statements reinforcing a sense of inadequacy, such as "Why do I always mess up?" or "What's wrong with me?" These thoughts perpetuate a victim mentality and close any possibility of finding solutions. Instead of generating insight or action, they amplify feelings of failure and disempowerment.

Overgeneralization transforms a single adverse event or experience into a universal truth. For example, after a failed project at work, you might think, "I'm a complete failure," or "I can't do anything right." This distortion turns specific moments of difficulty into all-encompassing statements that make you incapable of overcoming future challenges. Overgeneralization warps reality and traps you in a mindset that limits your growth and potential.

Catastrophizing is another common pattern in toxic narratives. When we catastrophize, we take a minor setback or challenge and magnify it to extreme proportions, imagining the worst possible outcome. For example, a small mistake at work might become a full-blown crisis in your mind, leading you to believe that your career is doomed or that you'll never recover from the error. Catastrophizing fuels anxiety and creates a sense of dread, often making situations seem far worse than they indeed are.

Recognizing the impact of language is central to understanding how toxic narratives work. The way we speak to ourselves has a profound effect on how we experience life. According to Lisa Feldman Barrett's Theory of Constructed Emotion, emotions are not automatic responses to stimuli but are shaped by language and past experiences. The words we use to describe our emotions and circumstances actively construct the emotional reality we live in. For example, labeling a task as "overwhelming" rather than "challenging" creates an emotional barrier that can make you feel powerless to act. On the other hand, shifting your language to more neutral or positive terms can lead to a different emotional response—one that empowers rather than hinders you.

Toxic narratives don't only affect your mental and emotional health; they also have physiological consequences. Chronic stress, caused by ongoing negative thought patterns, triggers the release of cortisol—a hormone that, over time, weakens the immune system and increases vulnerability to illness. Psychoneuroimmunology (PNI), the study of the interaction between the mind and the immune system, reveals that negative thinking can impair your body's ability to fight infections and recover from illness. Stress and toxic narratives keep the body in a heightened state of tension, leading to long-term physical consequences such as hypertension, cardiovascular disease, and chronic fatigue.

Transformative Approaches

Breaking free from toxic narratives is not only possible but transformative. Several approaches can help reframe these negative thought patterns, replacing them with healthier, more empowering ones.

Appreciative Communication is rooted in the principles of Appreciative Inquiry, a strengths-based approach developed by David Cooperrider and Suresh Srivastava. Instead of focusing on problems or failures, Appreciative Communication focuses on what's working well and what can be built upon. This approach encourages you to reflect on positive moments and growth experiences, fostering a narrative of empowerment.

For instance, instead of dwelling on what went wrong at the end of each day, ask yourself: "What did I do well today?" or "How did I grow from this experience?" This reframing allows you to see your strengths and achievements and build upon them, no matter how small. Over time, this habit of positive reflection creates a foundation for a more constructive internal dialogue, replacing toxic narratives with self-affirming ones.

Affirmations like "I handled today's challenges with grace" or "I am capable of learning and growing" help reinforce a growth mindset. By consistently focusing on your strengths and successes, you cultivate a more positive internal dialogue that supports your self-esteem and emotional well-being.

Neuro-Linguistic Programming (NLP), developed by Richard Bandler and John Grinder, is a framework that explores the relationship between language, thoughts, and behavior. NLP emphasizes the power of reframing, which involves changing how you interpret a situation by altering the language you use to describe it. Doing so can shift your emotional response and break free from limiting beliefs.

One effective NLP technique is to replace phrases like "I have to" with "I choose to." For example, instead of saying, "I have to finish this project," try saying, "I chose to complete this project because it aligns with my goals." This slight shift reframes the task as a conscious choice, creating a sense of autonomy and control.

Another valuable NLP strategy is to challenge your limiting beliefs. When you think, "I never succeed," ask yourself, "Is that true? When have I succeeded in the past?" This process of questioning disrupts the automatic acceptance of negative beliefs, allowing you to replace them with more accurate and balanced thoughts.

Nonviolent Communication (NVC), created by Marshall Rosenberg, offers a compassionate approach to communication that fosters understanding and empathy. NVC teaches us to express ourselves clearly and nonjudgmentally, focusing on observations, feelings, needs, and requests rather than criticism or blame. This approach can be applied not only in conversations with others but also in how we talk to ourselves.

For instance, instead of saying, "I always fail," you might use NVC principles to reframe the situation: "I didn't achieve my goal this time, and I feel frustrated because I value competence and success." By identifying your feelings and underlying needs, you create a space for self-compassion and growth rather than self-criticism.

Practicing NVC with yourself can help you transform toxic narratives into more constructive ones. It allows you to recognize your unmet needs without harsh self-judgment, fostering a healthier relationship with yourself and others.

Cognitive Behavioral Coaching (CBC), rooted in the principles of Cognitive Behavioral Therapy (CBT) and championed by figures like Dr. Aaron Beck and Albert Ellis, is based on the idea that thoughts, feelings, and behaviors are interconnected. In CBC, how you think shapes your emotional responses and actions. Changing how you interpret and think about situations can shift your behavior and emotional state.

For example, by replacing "I can't do this" with "I'm learning to do this," you shift your internal narrative from limitation to possibility, much like CBC encourages reframing. CBC also emphasizes differentiating between cognitive distortions (irrational thoughts) and objective realities (factual observations). Recognizing this distinction helps you understand when your thoughts are based on cognitive biases or distorted thinking rather than objective reality.

For instance, saying "I didn't meet my deadline" is a fact, while saying "I'm a failure" is an irrational cognitive distortion. CBC encourages you to challenge these distortions and replace them with more balanced, empowering beliefs, such as "I faced challenges with this deadline, but I can improve next time." This practice fosters resilience, clarity, and a more constructive mental framework.

Practical Strategies to Transform Toxic Narratives

The description of these models may inspire you to delve deeper into each. You can find everything from books to unique training programs. However, beyond the depth of these models, it is possible to highlight some core commonalities they offer for transforming toxic narratives and cultivating a healthier internal and external dialogue.

1. Focus on Small Wins: Instead of focusing on your perceived failures or shortcomings, take time each day to celebrate small successes. Acknowledging small wins like finishing a task or making progress can shift your perspective even if you didn't achieve everything you planned. Over time, this practice helps to build a more empowering narrative focused on growth.

2. Reframe Challenges: When you face a challenge, instead of seeing it as a threat or limitation, try to reframe it as an opportunity for learning and growth. Ask yourself, "What can I learn from this?" or "How can I use this experience to grow?" Shifting your mindset from defeat to curiosity opens up possibilities for problem-solving and resilience.

3. Question Your Beliefs: When you notice a toxic narrative surfacing, such as "I'm not good enough," pause and ask yourself, "Is this true?" or "Is there evidence that disproves this belief?" By challenging your limiting beliefs, you weaken their hold over you and create space for more empowering thoughts.

4. Replace Judgments with Neutral Observations: When you catch yourself making harsh judgments, practice shifting to neutral observations. For instance, instead of saying, "I'm terrible at this," try saying, "I'm finding this task challenging right now." This subtle shift in language reduces the emotional intensity of the situation and opens up space for constructive action.

5. Use Empowering Language: Be mindful of your language in your internal and external conversations. Words have power, and simple changes—such as replacing "I can't" with "I'm learning" or "This is impossible" with "This is a challenge I'll face"—can have a profound impact on your mindset.

How to Catch Toxic Thoughts Early

Learning to catch them as they arise is essential to transforming toxic narratives. To do this effectively, you must develop mental identifiers—internal signals that help you recognize when you fall into negative thought patterns.

1. Identify Key Triggers: Start by identifying the specific situations, people, or emotions that trigger toxic narratives. For example, do you often think negatively after a conversation with a critical colleague or when facing a new challenge? You become more aware of their origin by pinpointing the moments when these thoughts arise.

2. Recognize Toxic Phrases: Create a list of common toxic phrases frequently in your internal dialogue. Phrases like "I'll never succeed," "I always mess up," or "No one cares about me" are indicators of toxic narratives. When you notice these phrases surfacing, they serve as red flags, alerting you to a harmful thought pattern.

3. Develop a Mental Notification System: Once you've identified your triggers and toxic phrases, create a mental system to notify you when they arise. This could be a visualization, such as a stop sign, a flashing light, or an internal alarm that sounds when a toxic thought appears. These mental cues help you pause and become aware of the negative thought before it spirals out of control.

4. Replace the Toxic Thought: Once your mental identifier has alerted you to a toxic narrative, immediately replace it with a more constructive or neutral thought. For example, if you think, "I'm not good enough," counter it with, "I'm doing my best, and I'm improving." This process helps rewire your brain, gradually shifting your internal dialogue from negative to positive.

5. Reinforce Positive Habits: Practice catching and transforming toxic thoughts daily. Over time, this mental process will become more automatic, and you'll find it easier to shift your narrative in real time. Regular reflection on your progress will reinforce the habit of replacing negative thoughts with more empowering ones.

By identifying and transforming toxic narratives, you improve your mental and emotional well-being and take an essential step toward better physical health. A positive internal dialogue helps reduce stress and promotes healing, creating a holistic foundation for well-being.

Toxic narratives can feel deeply embedded in your psyche, but with conscious effort and the right tools, they can be transformed. By recognizing the patterns of overgeneralization, catastrophizing, and limiting beliefs, you regain control over your thoughts, emotions, and actions.

Visualization

Transforming Toxic Narratives

Reflect on the toxic narratives you identified in your mind map. Describe how you redrew these pathways and how they changed your perception.

Reflection questions

What toxic narratives did you identify in your mind map?
How did you redraw the pathways to change these narratives?
What emotions did you experience when changing these narratives?
How has your mind map changed after this visualization?

Chapter Ten

An Optimistic View

Nurturing the Mental Landscape

Imagine waking up with hope and openness each morning, where your words and thoughts create a vibrant, flourishing mental landscape. Positive narratives are crucial in shaping our experiences and perceptions, ultimately influencing our mental and emotional well-being. In this chapter, we will explore how nurturing an optimistic mindset can lead to profound changes in your life, supported by insights from neuroscience and psychology. We will also cover practical steps to cultivate and sustain positive thinking, harnessing the brain's remarkable ability to adapt and grow.

Positive narratives have revolutionized the field of psychology. The shift from treating mental illness to promoting well-being was spearheaded by pioneers like Martin Seligman, whose development of positive psychology underscored the power of constructive thoughts and affirmations. Positive psychology emphasizes human strengths and potential rather than focusing solely on pathology. This new approach highlighted the importance of fostering emotional resilience, happiness, and a fulfilling life rather than just mitigating mental illness. Seligman's work is grounded in the PERMA model—which stands for Positive Emotion, Engagement, Relationships, Meaning, and Accomplishment—as essential to a flourishing life.

The Benefits of an Optimistic Mindset

Research consistently shows that cultivating positive thoughts significantly enhances emotional well-being, satisfaction, and social connectedness. People who engage in positive self-talk and daily gratitude practices tend to experience lower levels of stress, anxiety, and depression. This positive outlook promotes greater creativity, productivity, and social engagement, contributing to overall success and life satisfaction. By shifting from a reactive mindset to one grounded in optimism, individuals can develop a more positive emotional framework, resulting in increased happiness and long-term fulfillment.

Optimism is not just a personality trait—it's a choice, a way of interpreting the world that can be cultivated through intentional practice. Research has demonstrated that positive thinking has a profound impact on both mental and physical health. Studies conducted by the Mayo Clinic and other leading institutions have found that optimistic people tend to live longer, healthier lives. They exhibit lower rates of cardiovascular disease, have better immune function, and recover more quickly from illness and surgery. These findings suggest that the mind-body connection is critical in health outcomes, with optimism as a protective factor against chronic conditions and disease.

In addition to its physical benefits, optimism has been shown to enhance psychological well-being. One particularly fascinating study from the University of Kentucky examined nuns' autobiographies, revealing that those who expressed more positive emotions in their writings lived significantly longer than their more pessimistic counterparts. This research highlighted the profound long-term health benefits of maintaining a positive attitude throughout life, reinforcing the connection between emotional states and longevity.

Positive thoughts also help reduce stress, which is a significant contributor to many health issues, including hypertension, digestive problems, and weakened immune function. Stress is often linked to the release of cortisol, a hormone that, when overproduced, can damage the body. When you think positively, your body produces fewer stress hormones, leading to lower blood pressure, better digestion, and improved sleep quality. As stress levels decrease, the body's ability to heal and repair itself increases.

Furthermore, studies from Harvard Medical School suggest that positive emotions and an optimistic mindset can boost heart health by improving circulation, reducing inflammation, and decreasing the risk of coronary artery disease. The combination of a healthier cardiovascular system, enhanced immune function, and quicker recovery times from illness underscores the tangible physical benefits of a positive mindset. This holistic connection between mind and body demonstrates how cultivating optimism can be a powerful tool for maintaining physical health and well-being.

The Neuroscience of Optimism

Neuroscience research has unveiled new insights into how the brain supports optimism. The prefrontal cortex, located just behind your forehead, is responsible for higher-order functions such as decision-making, problem-solving, and regulating emotions. When you engage in positive thinking, this region activates neural pathways associated with reward and motivation, triggering the release of neurotransmitters like dopamine and serotonin, which promote happiness, well-being, and motivation.

Positive thinking reinforces these neural circuits over time, making optimism a self-perpetuating habit. This process, often called neuroplasticity, suggests that the brain's structure and function can change and adapt throughout life in response to new experiences and intentional practices. This means that even if someone has been a lifelong pessimist, they are not doomed to stay that way. By consistently practicing positive thinking, individuals can rewire their brains to favor more optimistic thoughts, building resilience against stress and anxiety.

Conversely, negative thinking activates neural circuits associated with fear and anxiety, reinforcing stress responses. The amygdala, the brain's fear center, becomes more active, leading to a heightened sense of threat or danger, even in everyday situations. This overactivation of the stress response leads to chronic anxiety, which negatively affects both mental and physical health. However, by engaging in cognitive reappraisal—reframing negative thoughts into more positive or neutral ones—individuals can decrease the amygdala's overactivity and promote a calmer, more balanced emotional state.

The difference between optimism and pessimism lies in how people interpret life events. Optimists tend to view challenges as temporary and surmountable, believing they have the power to influence outcomes. For example, an optimist might think, "This setback is difficult, but I can learn from it and improve." Conversely, pessimists are more likely to see challenges as permanent and pervasive, often feeling powerless to change their circumstances. They might think, "I failed because I'm not good enough, and things will never improve." This difference in interpretation affects not only emotional states but also motivation, behavior, and overall mental health. Optimistic explanatory styles—focusing on attributing success to personal abilities and seeing failures as learning opportunities—promote resilience and foster growth.

Cultivating Positive Narratives

The power of positive narratives is transformative. They help foster resilience, emotional well-being, and a sense of possibility. The language we use in conversation and our inner dialogue creates vibrations that influence our mental, emotional, and physical states. According to Dr. Barbara Fredrickson, a leading researcher in positive psychology, positive emotions broaden our thought-action repertoires, encouraging creativity and problem-solving. This concept, known as the Broaden-and-Build Theory, suggests that positive emotions make us feel good at the moment and help build lasting psychological resources, such as resilience, optimism, and social connections.

Cognitive reappraisal, or reinterpreting negative experiences in a positive light, plays a crucial role in managing emotions. By recognizing a negative thought, reframing it, and integrating a new, more positive perspective, you can reduce the emotional impact of stressful situations. This practice has been shown to improve emotional regulation and increase activity in the prefrontal cortex, which helps balance emotional responses and promotes well-being.

Reframing is a powerful tool for cultivating positive narratives. For example, when faced with a challenging situation, ask yourself, "What can I learn from this?" or "How will this help me grow?" These questions help shift the focus from blame or frustration to learning and growth. This shift in narrative not only improves emotional regulation but also encourages a more proactive approach to challenges.

You can incorporate several simple, daily practices into your life to nurture a positive mental landscape.

Gratitude Practice: Practicing gratitude is a powerful way to shift your focus from what's lacking to what's abundant in your life. Robert Emmons, a prominent gratitude researcher, found that people who regularly practice gratitude report higher positive emotions, greater life satisfaction, and increased optimism. Keeping a gratitude journal or taking a moment at the end of the day to reflect on what you are thankful for can enhance your emotional well-being. Gratitude helps rewire the brain to focus on positive aspects, reinforcing a more optimistic mindset.

Positive Affirmations: Starting your day with affirmations can reinforce self-worth and motivation. Self-affirmation theory, developed by Claude Steele, suggests that when individuals reflect on their core values and positive attributes, they can better cope with stress and adversity. Identify moments when you think negatively and reframe those thoughts into empowering statements. For instance, replace "I'm not good enough" with "I'm capable and learning every day." This simple practice can shift your mental landscape and boost your self-esteem.

Visualization: Visualization is an effective tool for nurturing optimism. Imagine yourself achieving your goals and experiencing positive outcomes. Studies on mental imagery have shown that visualizing success activates the same neural pathways as experience, helping you feel more prepared and motivated. Picture the steps you will take, the obstacles you'll overcome, and the satisfaction of your accomplishments. Visualization strengthens motivation and increases self-efficacy—the belief in your ability to succeed.

Mindfulness and Contemplation: Spend a few moments each day observing your thoughts without judgment. Through formal meditation or informal mindfulness practice, becoming aware of your inner dialogue allows you to navigate negative thoughts more effectively. Mindfulness meditation, in particular, has been shown to increase gray matter in areas of the brain associated with emotion regulation, attention, and self-awareness. This practice fosters emotional regulation and a deeper connection to your mental landscape, helping you respond to challenges calmly and clearly.

Acts of Kindness: Small acts of kindness toward others can significantly improve your mood and reinforce a positive self-image. According to research on prosocial behavior, helping others fosters a sense of purpose and connection, contributing to overall well-being. Engaging in kind acts—whether offering a compliment, assisting a coworker, or spending quality time with loved ones—releases oxytocin, often called the "love hormone," which strengthens emotional bonds and fosters positive social interactions.

Reframing Negative Thoughts: When you think negatively, rephrase the thought in a way that opens up new possibilities. Instead of saying, "I'll never succeed," try, "I'm working on improving, and success takes time." This shift in perspective helps reduce feelings of defeat and encourages persistence. The more frequently you reframe your thoughts, the more your brain will reinforce these positive neural circuits, making optimism more automatic.

The Chemistry of Well-Being

The brain's neuroplasticity—its ability to reorganize and form new neural connections throughout life—allows us to cultivate optimism and rewire negative thought patterns. Hebbian learning, a principle of neuroplasticity, states that "neurons that fire together wire together." This means that the more we engage in positive thinking and self-talk, the more our brains will reinforce these pathways, making optimism a default mode of thinking.

Positive emotions are closely tied to the release of certain neurotransmitters and hormones. Here are some practical suggestions to activate these feel-good chemicals.

Serotonin: This neurotransmitter is essential for mood regulation and feelings of well-being. Adequate levels of serotonin are associated with calm, joy, and gratitude. Here are a few activities:

- **Morning Walks**: Sunlight exposure stimulates vitamin D production, aiding serotonin synthesis. A morning walk outdoors, even for 10–15 minutes, can lift your mood.

- **Soothing Music**: Calming, melodious music can stimulate serotonin release, fostering a sense of peace and joy.

- **Nature Connection**: Activities like gardening, hiking, or caring for pets help connect you to nature's rhythms, enhancing serotonin levels and creating a sense of contentment.

GABA: The Calming Neurotransmitter: The Gamma-aminobutyric acid (GABA) helps calm the nervous system, reduce anxiety, and promote relaxation. To increase GABA levels, consider:

- **Yoga and Tai Chi**: These practices encourage relaxation and mindfulness, promoting GABA production and reducing stress.

- **Reading Inspirational Books**: Engaging in uplifting reading material helps shift focus away from daily worries, allowing GABA to flow more freely.

Dopamine: This neurotransmitter is often called the "pleasure hormone" and is linked to motivation, confidence, and focus. To boost dopamine:

- **Brisk Exercise**: Activities like jogging or cycling can increase dopamine, giving you a sense of accomplishment and energy.

- **Listening to Motivational Music**: Upbeat, energetic music triggers dopamine release, enhancing focus and determination.

- **Challenging Hobbies**: Learning a new skill or engaging in a challenging hobby activates dopamine pathways, boosting confidence and resilience.

Oxytocin: This neurotransmitter strengthens emotional bonds and fosters positive social interactions. Here's how to cultivate it:

- **Group Activities**: Participating in group exercises or social events promotes oxytocin release, deepening feelings of connection.

- **Acts of Caring**: Simple gestures like cooking for loved ones or volunteering foster oxytocin production, nurturing positive relationships.

Endorphins: This neurotransmitter is released during creative or physical activities, acting as natural painkillers and mood boosters. To increase endorphins:

- **Outdoor Cycling**: Cycling in nature engages both body and mind, releasing endorphins and promoting well-being.

- **Creative Arts**: Engaging in artistic activities such as painting, writing, or sculpting stimulates endorphins, inspiring creativity and joy.

Transforming Your Mental Landscape

Clearing the mental landscape of negative thoughts and replacing them with positive narratives is a transformative process. It requires practice, intention, and patience. However, making small, consistent changes can cultivate a mental environment that supports your well-being and fosters resilience. Here are some final tips to keep in mind.

Set Intentions: Start each day by setting a positive intention. Whether it's gratitude, self-compassion, or optimism, setting an intention can help guide your thoughts and actions throughout the day.

Monitor Self-Talk: Be mindful of how you talk to yourself. When you notice negative thoughts creeping in, gently challenge and reframe them. Over time, this practice will shift your inner dialogue to a more positive narrative.

Celebrate Small Wins: Recognize and celebrate small achievements. Even the smallest victories deserve acknowledgment, reinforcing the belief that progress is possible.

An optimistic mindset is not about ignoring challenges or pretending everything is perfect. It's about focusing on what's possible, sound, and within your control. Nurturing positive narratives can transform how you experience the world, building resilience, emotional strength, and well-being. You can actively shape your mental landscape through gratitude, affirmations, visualization, and small acts of kindness, creating space for joy, peace, and growth. With these tools, you can take control of your inner dialogue, steer your thoughts toward optimism, and enjoy the lasting benefits of a more positive, hopeful view of life.

Visualization

Creating positive narratives

Reflect on the dark room you illuminated. Describe the new narratives you created and how you feel now.

Reflection questions

How did you turn on the light and begin to create new narratives?
What new stories did you create to replace the limiting narratives?
How do you feel now that the room is full of light?

Chapter Eleven

Hidden Mandates

Words Tied to History

We live within narratives intricately woven with words, beliefs, and mandates, many of which originate in our families and cultures. These hidden mandates, often expressed through language, can stimulate growth or trap us in cycles of inhibition and fear. In this chapter, you will explore how family and cultural mandates shape your life scripts and influence your decisions, behaviors, and sense of identity. You can move toward personal freedom and growth by learning to recognize, question, and transform these deeply rooted beliefs.

Family mandates are expectations, beliefs, and values transmitted from generation to generation. These mandates can be explicit, such as career choices or religious practices, or implicit, rooted in everyday language and behaviors. They are powerful because they are often internalized early, becoming part of our identity and worldview. Since these beliefs are passed on with a sense of authority and love, they are not easily questioned. Understanding these mandates and learning to differentiate which ones serve your well-being and which limit you is crucial for personal development.

The influence of family beliefs can be subtle yet profound. These beliefs often shape how we view ourselves and what we deem "success" or "failure."

For instance, if a family places a high value on academic achievement, an individual might struggle to feel accomplished unless they are constantly excelling in this area. The fear of not meeting family expectations can create an internal conflict between what is genuinely desired and what is expected.

Family Mandates in Action

You likely have many words and phrases that carry mandates from your history—powerful messages tied to your deepest need for belonging and acceptance. From a young age, fulfilling these mandates makes us feel worthy of our family's approval and love. This emotional connection reinforces the mandates, making them feel integral to who we are. John Bowlby's attachment theory illustrates how early interactions with caregivers create secure or insecure attachments, which can shape our beliefs and behavior in adulthood. Challenging these mandates can feel like a betrayal, risking rejection and the loss of family support.

Consider Cynthia, who grew up in a family that valued academic excellence above all else. Her parents' frequent statements such as "Education is the key to success" and "You have to be at the top of your class" instilled in her a relentless drive. While this helped Cynthia achieve academic success, it also caused her considerable stress and a fear of failure, limiting her ability to explore other interests and passions. This created a narrow framework for her life, as she believed anything less than perfection was unacceptable.

Or George, whose passion for the arts conflicted with his family's expectations. Feeling compelled to follow in his father's footsteps and join the family business, George was torn by the mandate: "Family comes first." This deeply ingrained belief made it difficult for him to pursue his dreams without feeling guilty and disloyal. As a result, George internalized a sense of obligation that suppressed his authentic self, leading to inner conflict between family loyalty and self-expression.

For Sarah, growing up in a conservative family with strict gender roles meant that her career aspirations in engineering were met with resistance. The belief that "Women should put family before career" was hard to challenge. These implicit gender expectations, rooted in societal norms, clashed with her aspirations and caused her to question her ability to succeed in a field dominated by men.

Questioning or abandoning family mandates is challenging because it involves confronting deeply held beliefs that shape one's identity. Erik Erikson's psychosocial development theory emphasizes the role of family and culture in shaping identity during adolescence and early adulthood. Family mandates create internal conflict because they often feel like non-negotiable truths. Disrupting these ingrained patterns can alter family dynamics, leading to the risk of conflict and fear of losing the support system that has been a security source.

However, the key to overcoming family mandates is balancing respect for family values while embracing individual autonomy. It is not about rejecting your roots but rather about integrating them to allow for personal growth and freedom. Acknowledging that family members' perspectives were shaped by their own experiences can help you empathize with these mandates, even as you redefine your path.

Cultural Mandates

Cultural mandates are the collective beliefs and values embedded in society that shape our perceptions, behaviors, and sense of normalcy. Like family beliefs, these mandates can be just as powerful, subtly dictating what is acceptable, desirable, or "successful." Cultural norms are often implicit and woven into the fabric of society through media, education, and social interactions. Albert Bandura's social learning theory underscores how individuals learn behaviors and norms through observing and imitating others in their culture.

For many, success is equated with material wealth and social status. Joseph, for example, grew up in a culture that idolizes financial success. He felt immense pressure to pursue high-paying careers, even if it meant sacrificing personal happiness and well-being. The mandate "Success equals wealth" guided his decisions, making him prioritize financial gain over his passions. Joseph's sense of identity became intertwined with external success measures, ultimately leaving him unfulfilled despite his material achievements.

In addition, cultural narratives around risk and safety often stifle growth. Lily, for instance, grew up in a family that valued stability and caution. Constant reminders to "Play it safe" and "Avoid risks" made her fearful of change and new opportunities. Despite her desire to travel and explore different cultures, Lily is stuck in a routine that seems safe but deeply unsatisfying. Cultural mandates, reinforced by her family, created an invisible but powerful barrier that limited her potential for self-discovery and adventure.

Strategies for Breaking Free from Hidden Mandates

To free yourself from the invisible traps of hidden mandates, it's essential to take conscious steps to identify and transform them.

Analyze the Value of the Mandates: Reflect on your beliefs and values. Ask yourself where they originated and whether they align with your authentic self. Are these beliefs still serving you, or have they become obstacles to growth? For example, reflecting on the statement "I must succeed" can reveal underlying fears and pressures internalized by external sources.

Reframe the Mandates: Question the validity of harmful beliefs and reframe them to support your growth. Instead of holding onto the belief "I must be perfect," challenge it by acknowledging that perfection is unattainable and that growth comes from learning and making mistakes. Reframe it as, "I strive to do my best, and it's okay to make mistakes." This shift allows you to embrace imperfection as part of the growth process.

Free Yourself from Family Baggage: Set boundaries with family members who impose limiting mandates. Communicate your needs and assert your right to follow your path. For instance, if your family expects you to pursue a particular career, openly discuss your passions and interests. Tell them that chasing your dreams is essential to your happiness and fulfillment.

Explore Other Perspectives: Engage with different cultures, communities, and viewpoints. Cross-cultural psychology shows how exposure to diverse perspectives can expand one's worldview and challenge limiting beliefs. Travel, read, or engage with communities outside your immediate circle to broaden your understanding and question cultural mandates that no longer serve you.

Accept the Discomfort of the Unknown: Growth often involves stepping out of your comfort zone and embracing uncertainty. Carol Dweck's research on growth mindset emphasizes the importance of viewing challenges as opportunities for development. Small steps toward new experiences, such as trying a new hobby or meeting new people, can help you break free from the confines of mandates and encourage personal transformation.

Create New Narratives: Use empowering language to create new stories that align with your values and aspirations. Replace limiting beliefs with affirmations such as "I am capable of creating my path" or "I deserve to pursue my passions." Narrative therapy, developed by Michael White and David Epston, suggests that we can reclaim agency over our narratives and reshape our identities by externalizing and rewriting our life stories.

Living with Mandates

Family and cultural mandates are part of our personal and collective history. They will not disappear completely, as they are deeply rooted in our upbringing and in the society in which we live. The key lies not in eliminating them but in learning to live with them in a way that doesn't limit our choices or actions. Psychologist Albert Ellis, founder of Rational Emotive Behavior Therapy (REBT), taught that challenging irrational beliefs can reduce the emotional disturbances they cause.

Living with mandates requires consciously choosing which beliefs and values you want to uphold and which you wish to release. For example, if you grew up believing that "Success is measured by financial stability," you might decide that success is about personal satisfaction and balancing your professional and personal life. It's not about ignoring the mandates but redefining what they mean to you and how they influence your decisions.

An effective way to approach living with mandates is through metacognition, the ability to consciously observe and analyze your thoughts. By practicing metacognition, you can catch mandates as they arise rather than becoming entangled. Mindfulness-based cognitive therapy (MBCT) exemplifies how metacognition can disrupt automatic thinking patterns, allowing you to question their validity. For instance, when you think, "I must follow this path because it has always been done this way," metacognition invites you to stop and question, "Is this the path I want to follow?"

Practical Exercises to Challenge Mandates

Here are practical steps you can take in your everyday life to challenge the influence of hidden mandates.

In the Car: Use the time during your commute to reflect on your automatic thoughts. Are they driven by internal mandates telling you to be productive, or are they genuine reflections of what you want to accomplish?

While Walking: Observe your internal conversations. If you think about responsibilities or expectations, ask whether they stem from family or cultural mandates or align with your true desires.

While Waiting in Line: Pay attention to your judgments or comparisons of others. Are these thoughts rooted in internalized mandates about success, appearance, or social standing? How can you replace these comparisons with compassion and self-awareness?

Releasing Mandates

The following exercise is designed to help you connect deeply with the significant figures in your life—those who have influenced your identity, values, and beliefs. It is a ritual that allows you to express gratitude for the values and teachings that have been helpful while saying goodbye to mandates or beliefs that you no longer wish to carry. You can perform this exercise with photographs, meaningful objects, or simply through mental imagery. You can do it in one session or dedicate individual time for each person over several days.

1. Prepare the Space: Before you begin, choose a quiet, comfortable place where you feel at peace. Prepare the space with elements that connect you emotionally. If you have photographs of the people you will address, place them in front of you where you can see them. Alternatively, you can use objects that belong to them. If you prefer to work with mental imagery, close your eyes and bring each person to mind.

2. Express Gratitude: Focus on a significant person from your past—parents, grandparents, mentors, or any other figure who has impacted your life. Look at their photograph, hold the object associated with them, or visualize their image in your mind. Take a deep breath and connect with the teachings, values, and shared moments important to you. You can say out loud or in your mind:

"I thank you for everything you have taught me. Thank you for the values you passed on, the lessons I've learned, and the moments we shared. I appreciate your [identify what you received from this person].*"*

3. Say Goodbye to Limiting Beliefs: Once you've expressed gratitude, say goodbye to the beliefs, mandates, or expectations that no longer serve you. This might include limiting beliefs about success, family expectations, or anything else that has weighed on you. You can say aloud or to yourself:

"Today, I say goodbye to the beliefs and mandates that no longer serve me. I free myself from expectations that do not belong to me and let go of what limits me. I am grateful for what you gave me, but I now choose my path."

As you say these words, imagine these limiting beliefs dissolving—like leaves falling from a tree or lifting weights off your shoulders. Feel the lightness of letting go.

4. Integrate the Experience: After saying goodbye to these mandates, please take a moment to visualize your life without them. How does it feel to be free? Now that you are no longer carrying those burdens, what new possibilities open up for you now? Embrace the sense of freedom and excitement that comes with choosing your path.

Chapter Twelve
Uncertainty
When You Are Speechless

Life's constant changes and surprises often disturb the stability of our inner landscape. The diversity of experiences, emotions, ideas, perceptions, and habits can be overwhelming. When confronted with the unknown, this intimate landscape becomes fragile. Our brain works incessantly to make sense of new stimuli, creating narratives to navigate the fog of unpredictability. In this chapter, you will learn how narratives shape our response to the unknown and the importance of recognizing the words and emotions with which we approach everyday uncertainty, ensuring we don't get caught in the inertia of ambiguity.

Transforming Perceptions of the Unknown

Let's first explore how the brain deals with uncertainty. The brain's neurobiological identification of new experiences begins with specific stimuli that activate detector neurons. These neurons transform the unknown into signals distributed through neural networks. The brain functions as a cooperative system, with each neuron acting as a member of more extensive networks through associative interactions. These interactions create global meanings from local signals, forming the basis of our understanding of everyday events.

When confronted with a new experience or unfamiliar events, neurons sort, filter, and transmit stimuli. Initially, the brain processes these signals randomly, with neurons communicating to decipher the meaning of the experience. Through repetition, these signals form specific patterns, reinforcing certain neural pathways. The brain does not store detailed information like a camera; instead, it retains fragments of data, emotions, and images, which it reconstructs into a coherent narrative when recalling them. This means that in new situations, uncertainty arises because there is no established correspondence between external phenomena and the brain's internal neural networks.

Our narratives construct the mental frameworks we rely on to interpret the unknown. To transform the inner landscape, we must expand these frameworks, becoming aware of the biases in our gaze and the limits of our interpretations. While some situations are entirely new, others have existed before us but were unseen. The unknown is often not an objective reality but an artifact of our limited perspective. Revising our narratives can expand the brain's ability to interpret and integrate new information into our understanding.

Change the Framing of Situations: One way to expand your inner narrative is to change how you frame situations. Move from being the center of your narrative and incorporate the perspectives of others involved in your daily dynamics. Stanford psychologist Carol Dweck's mindset research suggests that how we frame challenges determines our capacity for growth. Often, we see ourselves as the protagonists of a story, interpreting other people's actions as reactions to our presence. However, if you widen the lens and acknowledge that each person's response has roots in their history and interests, the situation gains more complexity.

Allow Open Endings in Your Narratives: Life rarely fits neatly into our stories. To embrace uncertainty, leave space for open endings in your narratives. Psychologist Jerome Bruner, a pioneer in the study of narrative psychology, emphasizes the importance of understanding that stories are not fixed but evolving. Accept that unknown events can expand your inner landscape and redefine the meaning of circumstances. Consider the possibility that people or situations you initially mistrust could eventually surprise you. Have you encountered someone you initially doubted, only to discover later that they became critical friends or allies? Holding open the potential for new interpretations allows you to adapt to changing circumstances without clinging rigidly to initial assumptions. This approach to narratives encourages a sense of curiosity rather than fear.

Update Your Affirmations: Your narratives form a mental house constructed with certainties that can either open or close you off to new experiences. Revisiting your established ideas and beliefs is essential for keeping this house flexible. The question is whether what you believe is still valid or needs updating to fit your current life context. Cognitive behavioral therapy (CBT) encourages questioning automatic thoughts and updating beliefs to align with reality. Just as a house needs repairs and updates to remain functional, your mind needs periodic reassessment to ensure the narratives it holds still serve your growth. For example, the belief that "I must always be in control" may no longer serve you in a life stage where adaptability and openness are more beneficial.

Release the Emotional Weight of Words: Words are powerful. They carry emotional weight and chemical connections in the brain. Some words trigger deep emotional responses due to their association with specific experiences. Neurobiologist Candace Pert has shown that emotions are stored as peptides in the body, making emotional responses to words visceral and physical. If a particular word or phrase creates negative emotions, it can send you into a cycle of destructive thinking. You can cut the link between the emotion and the words by identifying these emotional triggers. For example, if a temporary setback at work brings disappointment or frustration, it might spiral into a larger narrative of defeat. Instead, stop the narrative early and reframe the emotion. This practice allows you to shift from a temporary emotional reaction to a more balanced perspective.

Change Some Habits: Habits are subtle but powerful forces that shape our responses to the world. Introducing small changes to your routine can create opportunities for new experiences and perspectives. Psychologist Wendy Wood describes in her research on habit formation that habits are ingrained patterns of behavior that often function automatically. This automaticity makes it challenging to break free from routine. However, minor disruptions—like taking a different route to work or trying a new hobby—can trigger the brain to forge new neural connections and break the inertia of habit. Embracing these small changes can make the brain more adaptable to uncertainty and help you see the world with fresh eyes.

The Biases of Language

The language we describe experiences influences our perceptions and reinforces cognitive biases. Our brains are wired to categorize and simplify information to make sense of the world. This process, while efficient, can lead to cognitive biases, which are systematic deviations from rational judgment. Language plays a critical role in shaping and perpetuating these biases.

Confirmation Bias: It occurs when we favor confirming our beliefs and ignoring information contradicting them. The language we use can reinforce this bias. For example, if you describe an event using words that align with your beliefs, you are more likely to reinforce those beliefs, even if they are not entirely accurate. Statements like "This always happens to me" create a narrative of perpetual bad luck, ignoring the times when things go well. This bias limits our ability to see the bigger picture and recognize patterns that deviate from our assumptions.

Anchoring Bias: It refers to relying heavily on the first piece of information (the "anchor") when making decisions. The language used to present this initial information can shape perceptions and influence outcomes. For instance, if a doctor says, "This treatment has a 70% success rate," you might feel optimistic. However, if the same doctor says, "This treatment has a 30% failure rate," you may feel pessimistic despite both statements conveying the same information. The initial framing acts as an anchor that shapes your interpretation of subsequent information.

Stereotyping: Stereotyping involves generalizing about a group of people based on limited information. Language plays a crucial role in reinforcing stereotypes. Phrases like "All teenagers are rebellious" or "The younger generation lacks responsibility" create a biased lens through which you view individuals. These stereotypes can distort reality, preventing you from seeing people as individuals with unique traits and experiences. Recognizing the role of language in perpetuating stereotypes is crucial for dismantling harmful biases and promoting a more nuanced understanding of others.

Overcoming Biases

One must understand how language shapes one's perceptions to navigate uncertainty effectively. Addressing some of the following points can reduce the impact of biases and foster a more open-minded approach to the unknown.

Question Your Language: Be mindful of the words you use to describe your experiences. Do you use absolute terms like "always" or "never"? These words can exaggerate negative experiences and reinforce cognitive biases.

Instead of saying, "I always fail," try reframing it as, "I didn't succeed this time, but I can learn from it." This shift helps break the pattern of negative thinking and fosters a growth mindset.

Expand Your Vocabulary: Using more nuanced and descriptive language can reduce bias and help you see situations from multiple perspectives. For example, rather than categorizing a project as a failure, you could say, "This project was challenging, but I learned valuable lessons from it." Linguist Benjamin Lee Whorf emphasized the importance of language in shaping thought. Expanding your vocabulary can broaden your interpretations of events and reduce the influence of automatic biases. Learning new ways to express experiences allows you to break free from rigid thinking patterns.

The unknown is not something to fear but an invitation to expand your horizons. Examining the narratives you construct and the language you use to describe the world can shift your relationship with uncertainty. Life's unpredictability, while disconcerting, is also the source of its most significant growth opportunities. Embrace the power of your narratives and let them guide you toward a fuller, more enriching existence.

Visualization

Facing Uncertainty

Reflect on the uncertain path you visualized. Describe how you used your guidance to move forward and what you learned about your ability to handle uncertainty.

Reflection questions
What obstacles did you encounter, and how did you overcome them?
What did you learn about yourself as you moved along the path?
How do you feel about uncertainty in your life now?

Chapter Thirteen

NEXT STEPS

The Permanent Search

Congratulations on reaching the end of this transformative journey! Through these pages, you have explored the profound power of words to shape your growth and mindset. Each chapter has equipped you with tools, strategies, and practical exercises, enabling you to harness language as a positive force in your life—promoting self-esteem, enhancing well-being, and fostering a more optimistic outlook. But the journey is far from over. It is, in fact, just the beginning of a life-long commitment to growth, exploration, and the unfolding of your true potential.

From the very beginning, you ventured deep into the intricate pathways of your inner dialogues, discovering how the words you choose to speak to yourself can profoundly influence your identity, self-worth, and overall well-being. By learning to identify and transform negative thoughts into narratives of empowerment, you've unlocked the ability to open yourself up to new possibilities. This process of rewiring your inner language is crucial—it's the foundation for reshaping the perceptions and behaviors that influence your reality. By modifying the way you talk to yourself, you have taken an essential step toward creating a more positive, meaningful life built on the bedrock of self-compassion and intentional growth.

These tools have given you the strength to reframe even the most challenging dialogues—whether with family, friends, or colleagues. You've learned to approach difficult conversations not as a source of conflict but as an opportunity for growth and connection. You now understand that effective communication doesn't mean avoiding discomfort but navigating it with empathy, assertiveness, and grace. Rather than alienating you from others, these skills serve as bridges to strengthen your relationships and deepen mutual understanding. You've also mastered the art of virtual dialogues in an era where digital communication reigns supreme. Even through a screen, your words carry weight, and you've gained the tools to navigate these interactions with mindfulness, ensuring that every conversation builds connection rather than disconnect.

Along the way, you confronted the corrosive effects of toxic narratives—the inner stories that drain your energy, undermine your confidence and cast shadows over your mental and emotional health. Recognizing and dismantling these harmful stories has been a pivotal step in your transformation. You now possess the insight to rewrite your internal narratives and replace limiting beliefs with affirmations of strength, resilience, and potential. You've realized that language doesn't just mirror your inner world; it actively shapes it. By consciously choosing words that foster growth, positivity, and resilience, you've redefined your mental landscape, setting the stage for a life of greater fulfillment and possibility.

Assertiveness, a cornerstone of this journey, has emerged as a guiding principle. Through assertiveness, you've learned the importance of communicating your needs, desires, and boundaries with clarity and self-respect while also honoring the perspectives of others. It's about balance—expressing yourself honestly while preserving the integrity of relationships. This newfound assertiveness is not merely a tool for self-expression; it is the foundation upon which stronger, more authentic connections are built.

However, this journey doesn't end here. As you refine your internal and external dialogues, remember the importance of your chosen words. Positive dialogue must become an ongoing practice, a habit that deepens over time. Words are not just how we express our thoughts; they are the building blocks of our mindset, the energy we send into the world, and how we navigate life's challenges. Gratitude, appreciation, and compassion should be at the heart of this practice. By choosing words that nurture relationships and foster authentic connections, you create the conditions for more profound personal and professional relationships.

In every conversation, whether with yourself or with others, you hold the power to create a positive impact. You can build bridges of understanding, strengthen bonds of love and friendship, and transform your inner landscape into one that is open, vibrant, and full of possibility. The choice of words, the tone of voice, and the intention behind your communication are all forces that shape your reality and the realities of those around you.

As you move forward, continue to use these tools. Remember that the language you choose is your greatest ally in moments of doubt or challenge. Words can lift you, push you forward, and guide you through life's uncertainties with confidence and grace. Real, lasting change begins with the words you choose and the meaning you ascribe to them. By caring for your inner language, you are planting the seeds of a life filled with meaning, purpose, connection, and joy. The words you speak to yourself and others create the future you step into—each word holds the potential to guide your actions, strengthen your resolve, and brighten your path.

Positive, intentional language is not just a tool for navigating difficult moments—it's a lifestyle. It's a way of showing up with integrity, courage, and purpose. And as you continue to cultivate these enriching dialogues, you'll find that the possibilities for growth are limitless. Conversations with yourself will become moments of reflection and development, while interactions with others will become opportunities for connection, understanding, and collaboration.

By now, you've also experienced how every word can catalyze change, a spark of inspiration that lights the way forward. Positive thinking and language are contagious. As you continue to walk this path, you will inspire others with your presence, clarity, and ability to uplift and encourage. This ripple effect can transform not just your world but the world of those around you. You have become an architect of possibility, crafting a life where optimism, compassion, and self-awareness are the foundation stones.

Remember that the path of growth is a journey, not a destination. There will always be new challenges, narratives to rewrite, and growth opportunities. But with the tools you've cultivated in this book, you have everything you need to move forward confidently. You have already proven that you can profoundly transform, and now it's time to take those lessons into the world and live them fully.

As you move forward, keep cultivating these positive and enriching dialogues. Continue to challenge and transform limiting beliefs, invite new perspectives, and seek conversations that align with your values and aspirations. Doing so will empower you to live a more fulfilled, purposeful life. Every word is a choice. Every conversation is an opportunity. Let your words be the light that illuminates your path, guiding you toward a future brimming with personal growth and meaningful connections.

Congratulations on the remarkable progress you've made so far. May every word you choose propel you into new dimensions of growth, empowerment, and joy. The journey continues, and with every step, you are moving closer to the life you were meant to live—full of meaning, purpose, and endless possibilities. Keep exploring, growing, and speaking words that elevate, inspire, and transform.

Chapter Fourteen
Online Resources

Below, you will find a series of applications and software to continue your exploratory process. They all have free access; some have paid plans with more features. Not all applications are in English, but you can still use the features.

Aura (www.aurahealth.io) is a mental wellness platform that offers personalized meditations, sound therapies, and mindfulness exercises to help you reduce stress and improve your emotional health. It also features bedtime stories and gratitude tools tailored to your daily needs.

Daylio (www.daylio.net) is a visual diary app that allows you to record your mood and daily activities without writing. You can also track emotional patterns and habits with graphs and statistics to consciously improve your well-being.

Calm (www.calm.com) is one of the most popular meditation and sleep apps. It offers guided meditations, bedtime stories, and breathing programs to reduce stress and promote relaxation.

Happify (www.happify.com) uses science-based games and activities to help you improve your emotional well-being and build positive habits. The platform offers personalized pathways to build resilience, manage stress, and increase happiness.

Morning Pages (www.morningpages.app) is designed to help you practice daily writing in a structured way, following Julia Cameron's "morning pages" technique. Writing without interruptions every morning lets you free your mind and fosters creativity.

Penzu (www.penzu.com) is a free online diary where you can record your thoughts and emotions daily. It allows you to keep track of your reflections securely and privately.

Google Keep (keep.google.com) is a simple, free tool from Google for taking quick notes and keeping a digital diary. You can use it to record daily words and reflections.

ThinkUp (www.thinkup.me) is a free app that lets you record and listen to personalized positive affirmations. It is ideal for reinforcing positive thoughts every day.

Affirmation Pod (www.affirmationpod.com) is a free podcast that offers positive affirmations and guided meditations. It is great for reinforcing affirmations daily.

Healthy Minds (https://hminnovations.org/meditation-app): created by Healthy Minds Innovations, develops an app that offers a series of guided meditations and practices for emotional and mental well-being based on scientific research. Focusing on neuroscience and contemplative practice, the app helps users develop skills such as concentration, social connection, sense of purpose, and resilience.

The Gratitude App (www.gratefulness.me) helps you focus your language on gratitude and the positive by recording what you are grateful for daily. This can help you become more aware of the language you use.

Replika (www.replika.com) is an artificial intelligence chatbot that helps you have more conscious conversations and practice positive rephrasing in real time.

Coursera (www.coursera.org) offers free personal development, wellness, and positive psychology courses. You can also join communities that focus on personal growth.

Insight Timer (https://insighttimer.com/) is a free meditation and mindfulness app with thousands of guided meditations and podcasts that promote wellness and positive thinking.

Goodreads (www.goodreads.com) is a free platform for discovering inspirational and motivational books. You can create reading lists of books that promote positive language and thinking.

Smiling Mind (www.smilingmind.com.au) is a free app that offers meditation and mindfulness programs designed to reduce stress and improve emotional awareness.

Headspace (www.headspace.com) is a paid app that offers a selection of free meditations to help you incorporate mindfulness practices.

Padlet (www.padlet.com) is a popular platform for creating virtual murals. You can add notes, images, links, and more. It is ideal for organizing thoughts, visualizing narratives, and carrying out narrative exercises.

Miro (www.miro.com) is an online collaborative whiteboard that allows you to create mind maps, murals, and diagrams. It is an excellent option for visualizing your statements, thoughts, and narratives in an interactive space.

Milanote (www.milanote.com) is a visual organization tool for creating boards for creative projects. It is ideal for capturing thoughts, statements, and new narratives aesthetically pleasingly.

THANK YOU!

I thank you for exploring these ideas.

It is a great satisfaction for me to provide inspiring perspectives for your life. I hope I have fulfilled my goal of motivating the new in your life.

If you think this book has been helpful to you, it would be precious for me to hear about your experience. Please take a few minutes to leave a comment to let me know how your experience has been and to allow others to approach these ideas.

You can use the following link or QR code to submit your comment.

Chapter Fifteen
REFERENCES

Bandura, A. (1997). *Self-efficacy: The exercise of control*. W.H. Freeman.

Barrett, L. F. (2006). *Solving the emotion paradox: Categorization and the experience of emotion*. In *Emotion and Consciousness* (pp. 25-50). Guilford Press.

Barrett, L. F. (2017). *How emotions are made: The secret life of the brain*. Houghton Mifflin Harcourt.

Beck, A. T., & Alford, B. A. (2009). *Depression: Causes and treatment* (2nd ed.). University of Pennsylvania Press.

Berkovich-Ohana, A., & Glicksohn, J. (2017). The consciousness state space (CSS)—A unifying model for consciousness and self. *Frontiers in Psychology*, 8, 1961.

Boccia, M., Piccardi, L., Palermo, L., Nori, R., & Palmiero, M. (2015). Where do bright ideas occur in our brain? Meta-analytic evidence from neuroimaging studies of domain-specific creativity. *Frontiers in Psychology*, 6, 1195.

Bohm, D. (1996). *On dialogue*. Routledge.

Brown, B. (2012). *Daring greatly: How the courage to be vulnerable transforms the way we live, love, parent, and lead*. Avery.

Bruner, J. (1991). The narrative construction of reality. *Critical Inquiry*, 18(1), 1-21.

Burns, D. D. (1989). *The feeling good handbook*. Penguin Books.

Creswell, J. D., Way, B. M., Eisenberger, N. I., & Lieberman, M. D. (2007). Neural correlates of dispositional mindfulness during affect labeling. *Psychosomatic Medicine*, 69(6), 560-565.

Csikszentmihalyi, M. (1990). *Flow: The psychology of optimal experience*. Harper & Row.

Damasio, A. R. (1994). *Descartes' error: Emotion, reason, and the human brain*. Putnam.

Davidson, R. J., & Begley, S. (2012). *The emotional life of your brain: How its unique patterns affect the way you think, feel, and live—and how you can change them*. Penguin.

Davidson, R. J., & McEwen, B. S. (2012). Social influences on neuroplasticity: Stress and interventions to promote well-being. *Nature Neuroscience*, 15(5), 689-695.

Deci, E. L., & Ryan, R. M. (2008). *Self-determination theory: A macrotheory of human motivation, development, and health*. Canadian Psychology, 49(3), 182–185.

Denny, B. T., Kober, H., Wager, T. D., & Ochsner, K. N. (2012). A meta-analysis of functional neuroimaging studies of self- and other judgments reveals a spatial gradient for mentalizing in medial prefrontal cortex. *Journal of Cognitive Neuroscience*, 24(8), 1742-1752.

Duckworth, A. L. (2016). *Grit: The power of passion and perseverance*. Scribner.

Ekman, P. (2003). *Emotions revealed: Recognizing faces and feelings to improve communication and emotional life*. Henry Holt and Co.

Epstein, S. (1994). Integration of the cognitive and the psychodynamic unconscious. *American Psychologist*, 49(8), 709–724.

Farb, N. A., Segal, Z. V., & Anderson, A. K. (2013). Mindfulness meditation training alters cortical representations of interoceptive attention. *Social Cognitive and Affective Neuroscience*, 8(1), 15-26.

Feldman Barrett, L., & Satpute, A. B. (2013). Large-scale brain networks in affective and social neuroscience: Towards an integrative functional architecture of the brain. *Current Opinion in Neurobiology*, 23(3), 361-372.

Fredrickson, B. L. (2001). *The role of positive emotions in positive psychology: The broaden-and-build theory of positive emotions.* American Psychologist, 56(3), 218–226.

Frewen, P., Evans, E. M., Maraj, N., Dozois, D. J., & Partridge, K. (2008). Letting go: Mindfulness and negative automatic thinking. *Cognitive Therapy and Research*, 32(6), 758-774.

Gallagher, S. (2000). Philosophical conceptions of the self: Implications for cognitive science. *Trends in Cognitive Sciences*, 4(1), 14-21.

Gazzaniga, M. S. (2000). Cerebral specialization and interhemispheric communication: Does the corpus callosum enable the human condition? *Brain*, 123(7), 1293-1326.

Goleman, D. (1995). *Emotional intelligence*. Bantam Books.

Gottman, J. M., & Silver, N. (1999). *The seven principles for making marriage work*. Three Rivers Press.

Gross, J. J. (2002). Emotion regulation: Affective, cognitive, and social consequences. *Psychophysiology*, 39(3), 281-291.

Hayes, S. C., Strosahl, K. D., & Wilson, K. G. (1999). *Acceptance and commitment therapy: An experiential approach to behavior change*. Guilford Press.

Holzel, B. K., Lazar, S. W., Gard, T., Schuman-Olivier, Z., Vago, D. R., & Ott, U. (2011). How does mindfulness meditation work? Proposing mechanisms of action from a conceptual and neural perspective. *Perspectives on Psychological Science*, 6(6), 537-559.

Kahneman, D. (2011). *Thinking, fast and slow*. Farrar, Straus, and Giroux.

Kross, E., & Ayduk, Ö. (2011). Making meaning out of negative experiences by self-distancing. *Current Directions in Psychological Science*, 20(3), 187-191.

Lazarus, R. S., & Folkman, S. (1984). *Stress, appraisal, and coping*. Springer.

LeDoux, J. E. (1996). *The emotional brain: The mysterious underpinnings of emotional life*. Simon & Schuster.

Lieberman, M. D. (2007). Social cognitive neuroscience: A review of core processes. *Annual Review of Psychology*, 58, 259-289.

Maslow, A. H. (1954). *Motivation and personality*. Harper.

Merton, R. K. (1968). *Social theory and social structure*. Free Press.

Neff, K. D. (2011). *Self-compassion: The proven power of being kind to yourself*. William Morrow.

Northoff, G., Heinzel, A., de Greck, M., Bermpohl, F., Dobrowolny, H., & Panksepp, J. (2006). Self-referential processing in our brain—A meta-analysis of imaging studies on the self. *NeuroImage*, 31(1), 440-457.

Ochsner, K. N., & Gross, J. J. (2005). The cognitive control of emotion. *Trends in Cognitive Sciences*, 9(5), 242-249.

Oxytocin Research Institute. (2017). *Oxytocin: The hormone that bonds us*. Neuroscience Publications.

Panksepp, J. (1998). *Affective neuroscience: The foundations of human and animal emotions*. Oxford University Press.

Peterson, C., & Seligman, M. E. P. (2004). *Character strengths and virtues: A handbook and classification*. Oxford University Press.

Rogers, C. R. (1961). *On becoming a person: A therapist's view of psychotherapy*. Houghton Mifflin.

Rosenthal, R., & Jacobson, L. (1968). *Pygmalion in the classroom: Teacher expectation and pupils' intellectual development*. Holt, Rinehart & Winston.

Seligman, M. E. P. (1991). *Learned optimism: How to change your mind and your life*. Knopf.

Seligman, M. E. P. (2018). *The hope circuit: A psychologist's journey from helplessness to optimism*. PublicAffairs.

Siegel, D. J. (2010). *Mindsight: The new science of personal transformation*. Bantam.

Siegel, D. J. (2001). Toward an interpersonal neurobiology of the developing mind: Attachment relationships, "mindsight," and neural integration. *Infant Mental Health Journal*, 22(1-2), 67-94.

Vygotsky, L. S. (1986). *Thought and language* (A. Kozulin, Trans.). MIT Press.

Watzlawick, P., Weakland, J. H., & Fisch, R. (1974). *Change: Principles of problem formation and problem resolution*. Norton.

Made in the USA
Columbia, SC
09 January 2025